# PASSING WARM-UPS

## Direct from Guardiola, Simeone, Ancelotti, Emery, Sarri & Heynckes

### Written by

**Fausto Garcea**

**Daniele Zini**

### Published by

# PASSING WARM-UPS

## Direct from Guardiola, Simeone, Ancelotti, Emery, Sarri & Heynckes

**First Published in English - December 2021 by SoccerTutor.com**
**First Published in Italian - Aprile 2018 by Allenatore.net S.A.S.**

**info@soccertutor.com | www.SoccerTutor.com**

**UK:** 0208 1234 007 | **US:** (305) 767 4443 | **ROTW:** +44 208 1234 007

**ISBN:** 978-1-910491-53-9

**Authors:** Fausto Garcea and Daniele Zini

**Editor:** Alex Fitzgerald - SoccerTutor.com

**Diagrams Design by SoccerTutor.com**
All diagrams in this book have been created using Tactics Manager Software
- available from www.SoccerTutor.com

**Cover Design:** Alex Macrides, Think Out Of The Box Ltd.
Email: design@thinkootb.com Tel: +44 (0) 208 144 3550

**Note:** While every effort has been made to ensure the technical accuracy of the content of this book, neither the author nor publishers can accept any responsibility for any injury or loss sustained as a result of the use of this material.

# CONTENTS

# CO-AUTHOR: FAUSTO GARCEA

- **UEFA 'B' Licence**

- **Technical Manager** of the Football School at San Giuliano FC, which is the **Technical Centre of FIGC (Italian Football Federation)** and has a training affiliation with **Atalanta B.C**.

- **Youth Team Manager** at San Giuliano FC (Pisa)

## QUALIFICATIONS

- **Professional Athletic Trainer** (Italian Football Federation - FIGC Coverciano Federal Technical Centre)

- **Professional Sporting Director** (Italian Football Federation - FIGC Coverciano Federal Technical Centre)

- **TFA Teacher Degree in Motor Science**

- **Teacher** for the **Italian National Olympic Committee (CONI)**

- Teacher at Tuscany Sports School

## PREVIOUS COACHING ROLES

- **Technical Manager** of the Empoli Football School 2005-14

- Experienced **Youth Coach** in various positions in the sectors of Lucchese and Pisa

## PREVIOUS PUBLICATIONS

- **Author** of books and publications including "Football: Knowing it in order to teach it" and "Empoli workshop."

- **Co-author** of several publications, including "Empoli Giovani FC. Technique, tactics, coordination in the youth sector," "Football; the evaluative tests of conditional and coordination skills for amateurs and the youth sector" and "Train the reading of spaces."

*"To my great friends and companions in adventure Stefano, Paolo, and Sauro who stopped running after a ball too soon."*

## There is nothing sadder than a deflated football...

*Edson Arantes do Nascimento, Pelé.*

*Fausto Garcea*

# CO-AUTHOR: DANIELE ZINI

- **UEFA 'A' Licence**

- **Head Coach** for S.G. Cagliari Calcio Under 17

- **Head of Methodology and Training** for S.G. Cagliari Calcio

## QUALIFICATIONS

- After first securing the UEFA 'B' Licence, Daniele obtained his **UEFA 'A' Licence** in 2017 at the **FIGC Coverciano Federal Technical Centre** (central training ground and technical headquarters of the Italian Football Federation)

- Ranked 1st in the **Level 1 Course to coach Futsal**

## PREVIOUS COACHING ROLES

- **Manager and Technical Director** at U.S. Città di Pontedera

- **Head of Empoli Coaching Affiliates**

- **Football Camp Coach** for Empoli F.C., AC Milan, R.S.C. Anderlecht and Pontedera

- **Assistant Coach** at Sanluri (Serie D)

- **Youth Coach** at Valdera Calcio, Pisa Calcio, Us Ponsacco, and Pontedera Football

## PLAYING CAREER

- Youth player in the sectors of Pisa and Empoli

- Player in **Serie C** and **Serie D** until a serious injury forced Daniele to retire from football very early in his career

- At the age of 30, Daniele started again with a new adventure in Futsal, where he was a star with Palmares, scoring almost 200 goals, and winning 5 promotions up to the Serie B division

**PASSING WARM-UPS**

*I have a special thank you to my father who has not been around for a long time, to my mother, to my family, to the women of my life, Valeria, and to the little Noemi and Viola.*

*Thanks go to all the clubs, to the executives who believed in my philosophy, in my ideas, in my concepts, in my principles and in my abilities.*

*Thanks to all the players I have trained, as thanks to you I have acquired self-awareness, experience, trust, and security, I learned to keep relationships, compare, experiment, edit and expand my knowledge.*

*Thanks to Martino Melis, a friendship born on the first school desks and on the football fields after.*

*A special thanks to Maurizio and Marcello Pantani and the whole Pantani family for having always demonstrated their trust and esteem.*

*Thanks to all the members of the U.S. Città di Pontedera who helped me realise the dream of obtaining the UEFA A diploma and becoming a professional coach.*

*Thanks to the municipal administration of Pontedera, in particular to Mayor Millozzi and to the Franconi Sports Councilor for always being available and close to the U.S. Città di Pontedera and the youth sector of the U.S. Città di Pontedera.*

*Thanks to Elio Ferri and Luca Franceschi (AS Roma) who asked me to start more than 20 years ago to coach the football school in my country.*

*Thanks to Luciano Spalletti (current Napoli manager) and all his staff.*

*Thanks to Marco Domenichini (current Napoli assistant manager), who has always been close to me since I started all my adventures.*

*Thanks to Massimiliano Cappellini, Moreno Simonetti, Fausto Garcea and Antonio Cernicchiaro, for me you are like a second family.*

*Thanks to Vito Consoloni, Sergio Giuntini, and Alessandro Balluchi.*

*Thanks to Vincent my spiritual "guru," to Giovanna Catizone, VinceJr and Alessandra for the fantastic experience, to Eddie Rossman my football brother from Staten Island (New York), to Joe Correale, Cosimo, Rosemarie, Maryann, Anthony, Alyssa for all they have made for me. To the president coaches, Renzo Ulivieri, a man who with his football passion makes his lectures to the teachers he teaches unique, extraordinary, and indescribable. They passed on their experiences, skills, and knowledge throughout the UEFA A course at Coverciano Federal Technical Centre, which is the best coaching school in the world.*

**Daniele Zini**

# DIAGRAM KEY

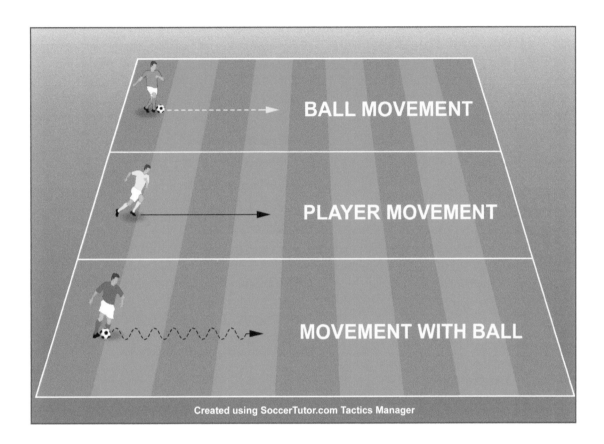

BALL MOVEMENT

PLAYER MOVEMENT

MOVEMENT WITH BALL

Created using SoccerTutor.com Tactics Manager

## PRACTICE AND TACTICS FORMAT

**Each practice or tactical example includes clear diagrams with supporting training notes such as:**

- Name of practice or tactical example
- Description of practice or tactical example
- Player actions
- Player movements

# INTRODUCTION

Each member of the coaching staff is, in equal parts, an "ethical" manager of the physical and mental condition of the players. The technical and tactical ability of each player and each team is entrusted to them.

In their daily duties on the pitch and in the preparation of each individual training session, **Fausto Garcea** and **Daniele Zini** have always been convinced that you must use all the scientific knowledge available to plan all activities before, during and after training and matches.

A basic part of training is the tactical-technical activation (warm-up). This book is made up of two parts that intertwine and merge. The first part, written by **Fausto Garcea**, analyses the basic principles of activation and warm-ups.

Training concepts and means such as activation and stretching are defined and described methods of exercises. There is also information on the dimensions and geometrical shapes used for warm-up practices, technical and tactical training, and modern theories such as mirror neurons, cognitive and motor learning.

Importance is also given to a common language, made up of keywords and analysis of the most common definitions of individual and collective actions specific to modern football.

The second part of the book, written by **Daniele Zini**, is the result of a long process to observe and learn the warm-up practices used by some of the world's best coaches:

- **Pep Guardiola**
- **Diego Simeone**
- **Carlo Ancelotti**
- **Unai Emery**
- **Maurizio Sarri**
- **Jupp Heynckes**

The book shows the technical-tactical warm-ups used by these coaches, which vary depending on their tactical ideas of development during the various phases of the game.

All of the warm-up practices from these six top coaches have a common characteristic, as they are the result of clear ideas, of precise and detailed programming.

Each coach's warm-up practices in this book are distinguished from the others by what they want from their players and team - different actions, movements, timings, dimensions, and shapes.

Of course, this book is a small and humble contribution to the world of football, but if a coach has the patience to read it, the content is applicable to every age, level, and environment.

# WARM-UPS: ESSENTIAL ASPECTS AND SCIENTIFIC FINDINGS

*Editorial recognition: photo-oxser / Shutterstock.com*

# WARM-UPS: ESSENTIAL ASPECTS AND SCIENTIFIC FINDINGS

The only objective of this section is to analyse the scientific principles and essential aspects for warm-up exercises/practices.

It is important not to underestimate this very important phase of the training session, as you could consequently "damage" the stages to follow.

All coaches are certainly able to plan and conduct a warm-up exercise/practice, but less coaches are capable of linking them to decision making and intelligent technical-tactical-motor skills.

The starting point is the search for the specificity of the situation, the adaptation, and the variables characterising a sport which, in its structural applications, thanks to the contribution of science, has become more complex.

For years we have been part of that "team of madmen" who thinks that the details are important; that read, study, analyse, try, make mistakes, study again, try again, fix. It is not "racking one's brains" but the only right way to approach football without missing key ingredients.

Before any sporting or non-sporting activity, each individual's body is calibrated and regulated physiologically on their base performance capacity.

The initial situation, the state of balance of body functions is **Homeostasis**. This is the moment we decide to "do something" and do it e.g. Swim in the sea or take a long walk - we subject our body to a series of stress.

Fatigue is the indicator to make us understand when homeostasis is destabilised and that the situation is now that of **Heterostasis** i.e. Temperature, heart rate and breathing have undergone a significant, sudden, immediate alteration far from regular levels. You can imagine that if this change is sudden, it is therefore dangerous, harmful, and destructive if it is not scientifically managed. For a sporting activity in general and/or football specifically, the transition from homeostasis to heterostasis needs to be closely monitored.

The warm-up, therefore, covers the task of preparing the various functions of the body and mind to a work capacity and superior performance, to better manage heterostasis and to prevent the shocks which can occur when moving from homeostasis to heterostasis. In addition to preventing injuries, adequate heating (warm-up) also serves to raise and strengthen the physiological, psychological, technical, and tactical qualities the players are to face in the following phase of the training session and/or competition.

If we go "deeper" into substantial changes, our locomotor system (skeleton, skeletal muscles, ligaments, tendons, joints, cartilage) is predisposed to various combined and complex movements. There are increases in body temperature (1.5 °), so that the risk of muscle strains can be lowered. The transport of oxygen in the blood increases as a consequence of the increase in respiratory rhythm and circulation.

The improvement in quantity and quality of the blood flow induces the activation of the muscle system in general and, specifically, of the affected muscle areas. There is a more rapid and profitable supply of oxygen to the muscles. The body increases the production of synovial fluid (joint lubrication), making the movement of the limbs safer and more beneficial.

For the nervous system, by accelerating the rate of transmission of the impulses, you obtain a better ability to respond quickly and learn by virtue of attention, concentration, and predisposition to the motor and/or technical act higher than the "Homeostasis" levels (base equilibrium). On a purely cognitive level, it represents a dynamic information puzzle (internal feedback) to prepare for the correct and economic execution of the technical actions.

In our work, we would not want to be overly concerned with minor details or overload the reader. However, we wish to provide general theoretical indications about what is commonly meant by heating or warming up.

First of all, we embrace the "globalised" idea of the three phases that make up a simple training session:

1. **Warm-up** (general and/or specific of the discipline)

2. **The Main Part** (specific of the discipline)

3. **Cooldown** (general and/or specific)

Prof. Enrico Arcelli is a pioneer who faced scepticism from many coaches, managers, and presidents. However, as an expert mentor of young physical education teachers and of young coaches, he distinguished three types of warming up:

1. **General**

2. **Specific**

3. **Passive** (with external heat supply i.e. Saunas, hot baths, etc.)

Passive warm-ups is only indicated among the possible alternatives but is not recommended. Indeed, it is "used" by Prof. Arcelli in his own dissertations in reference to scientific studies, that **warming up must always take place actively**, and also makes the point that warm-ups are always needed regardless of high temperatures in the summer months. This is because the only parameter that matters when talking about injury prevention and sports performance is the internal temperature of the body.

# Training Session and Pre-Match Warm-ups

*Editorial recognition: Cosminlftode / Shutterstock.com*

We embrace, for clarity and simplicity, the other "globalised" idea that there are two types of warm-up:

1. **Training Session Warm-up**
2. **Pre-match Warm-up**

The **TRAINING SESSION WARM-UP** can consist of exercises with general characteristics in regard to both the cardiovascular and respiratory systems, and the technical-tactical part.

They are **not required to have a greater load in quantity and intensity** of execution of movements/actions, motor skills and technical actions (we will see later what is meant by the concept of "load").

In this type of warm-up, the onset of a certain feeling of fatigue can be admitted only if adequately "weighed" and included in the total calculation of the effort.

The **PRE-MATCH WARM-UP** must contain elements aimed at the technical and tactical specifics that are required for the upcoming match.

In other words, it **needs to include situations that can be found and reproduced in the game**.

**Using the ball in pre-match warm-ups is essential**, in addition to the obvious use of the muscles and the general organic components.

The coach must set themselves and pursue the goal of absolute specialisation of technical actions, tactical movements, the correct body shape, and football motor skills.

This is all in addition to the continuous reference to the tactical strategies which are "stored" in the mind of each player in harmony with the coach and team's strategy.

However, the pre-match warm-up must also exclude the habits stored which do not fit the team's tactical plan for the game.

Although in recent years, things have been changing and everything is much more "accelerated and intense," there is no need to take risks, especially in the very young age groups and adolescents.

There is **no need to exaggerate training with excessive demands** on the mind or chemical processes.

It is better not to prematurely induce the accumulation of lactic acid, and/or prematurely weaken the concentration, attention, and response capacities, which are all skills that must be kept at maximum levels for as long as possible during a match.

# Training Session Warm-ups: Basic Principles

For a clear overview of the initial phase of the training session (warm-up), we want to outline basic principles to follow:

- The warm-up **must be appropriate to the climate/environment** e.g. Type of pitch - grass, hard synthetic ground, soft synthetic ground.

- The warm-up must also be **appropriate for the age** of the players, their **technical level**, **tactical understanding**, **motor skills**, **physical capabilities**, and their collective knowledge of what they are doing and what they are going to do.

- The **muscular groups involved must be identified** for each exercise and also recognise the type of injury prevention.

- **Injury prevention** - muscles should be treated individually and their mechanical function identified. Also note the types of muscle fibres and how they are composed, the energy characteristics, the rate of contraction and times of decontraction, the duration of the effort, and the need for elastic recovery.

- **Do not forget that muscles and joints form a whole** - the functional ability of one system is related and influences the functional capacity of another system.

Usually this is acknowledged at the time of a trauma/injury. An injured athlete realises the balance that exists between muscles and joints because the dysfunction of one leads to dysfunction of the other.

A coach does not have to wait for one of his players to get injured to be clear that a given muscle has a greater or lesser tendency to stretch, contract, or weaken during a particular stress.

Therefore, the balance with the affected joint or joints is there if that trend is respected. Otherwise, the alteration of this muscle-joint balance leads to trauma and injuries eventually.

A typical example in football, and especially in the youth sector and football schools, is the exact evaluation of the thigh muscles, which are continuously and excessively used in the typical action of "kicking the ball."

The quadriceps muscle group are the extensor of the leg on the thigh and knee and extend the knee joint. The quadriceps are a very strong and powerful muscle group that is biarticular, which means that the muscles cross two joints rather than just one. Together with the knee joint, the quadriceps also hold an important role for the **hip flexor**.

If this double mechanical function is not considered during the warm-up phase, not immediately but in the short and long term, the ischium-pelvic region (hip-pelvis) and the lumbar tract of the spine forces are unbalanced.

This will have negative consequences for weakening of the muscles of the buttocks and abdomen, which are necessary for players of all ages both in their motor actions and technical actions such as passing and/or shooting at goal.

At the same time, the systems and organs that allow the necessary energy (oxygen, fatty acids, etc) to be produced, maintained, and to complete the effort, as well as the work to eliminate waste products like carbon dioxide, lactic acid, superfluous heat, should not be underestimated.

In short, there is not a single "football model," but it is now clear that there are countless **"Performance Models."**

This is because there are many objectives to pursue, even in a 20 minute warm-up exercise at the beginning of a training session.

As we have experience in various sports fields (school, youth sector, football schools, advanced teams), we are led to say that a bit of healthy tradition never hurts.

In our humble opinion, in fact, a reasonable dose of mobility should not be overlooked. Joint and muscle elasticity need to be a key part of any warm-up.

These skills (joint and muscle **mobilisation**, as well as **stretching**) can also be solved through classic technical practices with the ball.

Later in the book, there are sixty examples of these with **technical-tactical passing warm-ups** from some of the world's top coaches:

- **Pep Guardiola**
- **Diego Simeone**
- **Carlo Ancelotti**
- **Unai Emery**
- **Maurizio Sarri**
- **Jupp Heynckes**

# WARM-UPS AND STRETCHING

**Stretching** is present in almost all warm-up training across different sports all over the world. We must consider this very carefully...

**Joint mobility** is the ability to perform movements with the maximum amount of movement allowed by the anatomical structures of the joints involved, with the aim of the best possible result.

In scientific literature, joint mobility is sometimes grouped among conditional capacities such as strength, speed, endurance, and even coordination skills (abilities).

### Joint mobility is limited by several factors, including:

- *The remarkable rigidity of the tendons and ligaments*
- *Contact with the nearby walls of the body, muscles, organs, and fat*
- *The resistance of the muscles that oppose the movement in question*

You can intervene in joint mobility with appropriate stretching exercises too by trying to improve tendon-ligament rigidity and muscular endurance.

A brief clarification is needed for the difference in the terms extensibility and elasticity. They are too often wrongly described as the same when discussing sports and physical activities.

**Extensibility** is the ability of the skeletal muscles, tendons, and ligaments to be extended or stretched when induced by an appropriate and "weighted" stimulus. It depends on the structural properties of the intracellular organisation (muscle tissue) and/or of the intercellular structural organisation. The quantitative and qualitative assessment of the extensibility of a muscle or a group of muscles should be in centimetres and millimetres, and not time. That is, we only have to "measure" the length of the stretch and it does not matter how long it takes the muscle fibres to return to the initial situation.

**Elasticity** is the almost exclusive property of skeletal muscles which allows an elongation produced by a very precise stimulus to return to the original situation when the stimulus ends. More specifically, it is the MTU (muscle-tendon unit) ability to elongate during the eccentric phase of the movement and to be able to carry out a concentric contraction phase in a very short time, transforming the potential elastic energy generated and preserved over the course of the movement into mechanical work of the first eccentric phase. To put more simply - in this case, the evaluation concerns time; the shorter the time it takes for the muscle recovery, the greater the ability (the degree) to be elastic.

**KEY POINT:** *When discussing stretching, it is more correct to think about extensibility and not elasticity.*

Bob Anderson proposed stretching to major American football and basketball teams in the 1960s. Later, there were contributions from other enthusiasts such as Solveborn Heyward. Thirty years later, Gilles I presented his intellectual convictions based on physiological and scientific principles, a movement both in the informal and formal practice of stretching, and a scientific debate on the advantages and disadvantages.

The advent of this wonderful training medium (whose basic concepts come from yoga, therefore with roots certainly much older), are actually not "tiring" for athletes, so at one point it seemed like the cure for all ills. Stretching after running, stretching before running, stretching without running.

We saw in the 1990s, with our own eyes, teams of young teenagers, but also of professional adults, replace any type of pre-main part of training and/or pre-activity with 20, 30, or 40 minutes of stretching. We have always heard across the years by convinced instructors, coaches and athletic trainers far more competent, prepared, and respected than the writer, leaning towards an exclusive and indiscriminate use of stretching. After the first severe damages caused to muscles, tendons and even bones, fortunately the debate on this topic has become more profound and today the thoughts are varied.

There is now a consensus that there are three starting points of the discussion (physiological certainties):

1. **Static maintenance in active stretching** of the stretching position (not to be confused with passive stretching)

2. **Mutual innervation** is involvement of both the agonist and antagonist muscles during any movement

**Agonist** muscles perform movements and contract while others relax. **Antagonist** muscles perform an opposite movement and interfere with the action. A typical example in football is the actions of kicking the ball. The extensor and agonist quadriceps femoris muscle contracts and the antagonist flexor biceps femoris muscle (back of the thigh) relaxes.

The type of double neuromuscular activation is possible with a natural strategy collaboration that agonist and antagonist muscles adopt. For each movement there is a simultaneous **co-activation** (co-contraction), at a high level for the agonist and at a very low level for the antagonist.

The mutual innervation mechanism is the basis of stretching techniques, because our organism must be able to be aware of which muscles are affected during the stretching exercise.

3. **Tension produced** during the stretches involves three structures: Connective tissue, the elastic elements of the sarcomere and the actin-myosin bridges.

A **sarcomere** is made up of two protein filaments (actin and myosin), which are responsible for muscle contraction. **Actin and myosin form cross-bridges** between the thick and thin filaments, and this movement slides the actin filaments and shortens the sarcomere - which then leads to muscle contraction.

If these three basic principles in theory will then be respected in practice, the effects are likely to be positive.

For many specialists, however, the use of **complete stretching sessions for sports disciplines whose performance model does not give mobility a fundamental role, produces negative effects**. Football is one of these, which is in contrast with gymnastics or rhythmic gymnastics for example.

Other scholars and specialists believe that stretching exercises are especially useful before and during the session for muscle strengthening. They favour the phenomenon of supercompensation, which is about obtaining a higher performance steep, but they are not equally useful as a specific method for a session dedicated to them.

**Supercompensation** is the post training period where the person has a higher performance capacity than they did prior to the training period.

There are others, also supported by scientific studies, who claim that **passive stretching while maintaining static posture reduces the level of rapid strength performance, strength resistance, speed, and even jumping ability**.

Finally, for years we have been talking about **stretch-tolerance**, which increases the athlete's capacity to get used to the pain and to endure higher stretches than necessary. The analgesic effect of stretching "would put the pain receptors to sleep," causing an increase in the so-called **pain threshold** with the risk of possible micro-traumas and various different injuries.

*In the end, we conclude that only stretching (on its own with no other components) is a definite no for football training!*

*Editorial recognition: Vlad1998 / Shutterstock.com*

# EXERCISES, DRILLS AND WARM-UPS

The overall training schedule is determined in all sports by the scheduling of competition (friendly matches, league matches, tournaments, local matches, regional matches, national matches, etc) and the general principles characterising the **"workload."**

The training session can aim to improve **fitness levels** but also maintain an adequate **physical condition** at a specific moment (preparatory, pre-competition, competition, or transition), have lower or higher intensity or load, or it can even have one simple aim of preventing physical and/or mental over-training.

In recent years, the commitments of the team and individual players has really become too much, and it is extremely difficult to manage. This is due to the increasing number of games driven by the football industry and business.

The coach always has to juggle the weekly schedule, which clashes with the basic physiological principle of work and rest (or rather, recovery). In our case, the **performance model must be football specific**.

It is necessary to know the motor skills and physical abilities perfectly (general coordination, special coordination, conditioning), which are needed to characterise the specific load volume and intensity. This is in order to stimulate, strengthen and consolidate in each technical, physical and/or tactical exercise/practice, or in the various combinations of them.

The body of the athlete (footballer) reacts to stimuli, adapts to the stimuli themselves. Coaches must continually "weigh" the load and recognise the adaptations and modifications of what is a real **complex functional system**.

The qualitative aspects of the performance are as important as the quantitative ones. The latter can and must be detected through evaluation parameters - first of all, intensity, and volume.

**At this point, here are some necessary definitions:**

**LOAD:** Set of stimuli induced by exercises conducted in training session (cumulative amount of exercise).

**EXTERNAL LOAD:** Set of exercises (stimuli) chosen and proposed according to the objectives to be pursued and achieved. Quantity (volume) and quality (intensity) are the characterising parameters.

**INTERNAL LOAD:** Reaction of the organism (complex system) in response to the external load. The changes, for better or worse, can be biological, mental, cognitive.

**VOLUME:** Number of stimuli inherent to the single exercise proposed or the whole session of work out.

Quantity - number of repetitions of a technical or motor action; number of series; distance or sum of distances covered.

**INTENSITY:** Quantity - Percentage of Kg used compared to the ceiling in a given exercise (e.g. Lifting weights); speed when running; height exceeded in the various jumps as a percentage of your maximum limit; number of possible repetitions of the technical or motor action in a set amount of time.

Quality - muscular and organic commitments with respect to maximum possible performance.

**DENSITY:** Expression of the temporal (time) relationship between execution and recovery.

It is "measured" precisely by time or percentage values with respect to the series of the individual exercise or complete training session.

**FREQUENCY:** Number of times the same exercise (stimulus) is proposed and actually conducted in a certain time period (day/s, week/s, month/s).

**EXECUTION DIFFICULTY:** Degree of difficulty (simple or complex) of the exercise and the stresses. For this parameter, it is sometimes possible to create a scale of standardised values (objective evaluation), and sometimes not (subjective evaluation).

The same exercises can result in different levels of commitment, depending on the environment, climate, terrain, your qualities, and that of the opponent.

**LOAD MANAGEMENT:** In the operational proposals with load management, age, gender, and physical level must always be kept in mind, as well as the technical level and tactical understanding of the individual player and the team.

# FATIGUE

The training load must have fatigue as a natural and physiological consequence. Fatigue is a natural alarm system. In a state of functional discomfort, there is a decrease in the functional power of an organ, of multiple organs, or of the whole organism. This is due to a certain amount of work (load), and the athlete recognises it as a negative reaction. However, fatigue is one of the necessary elements, for the work itself to be profitable - it leads to the consumption of energy reserves (fuel) and the production of waste products (catabolites).

Beyond the limit of physiological **endurance** we come to a **strain**, a phase in which injury is probable and almost inevitable.

# REGENERATION

Regeneration is the next process that occurs during the recovery phase of restabilising. Our organism (perfect machine), in normal conditions and in perfect physiological autonomy, sets in motion precise mechanisms to recreate the energy substances used and to dispose of waste substances.

However, the regeneration time is not the same for all types of substances. It is very important to know that glycogen consumed is not restored simultaneously in all organs. On the contrary, in the vital organs (heart and brain), and also in the affected and stressed skeletal muscles from the activity carried out, the reconstruction is faster than e.g. The liver, which is a very important organ but slower in reconstruction.

**Lipid Oxidation** (fat consumption) represents the main source of restoration energy, and this reset does not bring the "quantity of fuel" to the starting level, but to a higher quantity, which is a very precious little reserve in case of a subsequent higher request, a more tiring workload than the previous one. This modus operandi (particular way or method of doing something) of our organism after stress is the basic principle of improvement of performance: **supercompensation** (D. Harre, 1977).

Intensity and efficiency of the regeneration processes and the duration (time) of the process are linked to each other and depend on the intensity of the **decomposition** of used substances and waste substances.

Faster and "better" will be decomposition, just as fast and positive will be **regeneration**.

SUPERCOMPENSATION: Post-training period where the athlete/player has a higher performance capacity than they did before the training started. The effects sought are created by the training session (exercises, work phases and recovery phases).

In other words, through adequate stimuli (mild and continuous, medium intensity, high intensity) we try to establish both the adaptation and the consequent right response to loads and stress, providing the ability to withstand greater stresses over time.

According to the aforementioned Dietrich Harre (point of reference for the studies concerning the training theories), supercompensation occurs fairly quickly in athletes who are in the initial phase of training and subjected to unusual loads.

For those athletes who have already achieved the maximum of their physical-organic-muscular potential, the supercompensation process can last weeks or even months. This phenomenon is recognised and defined by L. P. Matveev (Russian scientist, believed founder of sports training) as **delayed transformation**. This can prevent precise, continuous, and progressive information on the effects of the "load," stopping the trainer/coach from having clear and meaningful feedback.

For supercompensation to be progressive, systematic and in line

with expectations, loads must be high but, at the same time, suitable for the situation. The situation, monitored, controlled, and assessed on an ongoing basis, in turn needs loads that are not excessively standardised, but also not too fluctuating and uneven.

# OVERTRAINING

Otherwise, with inadequate and excessive stimuli, the onset of the **overtraining phenomenon**, which despite the term probably leading to optimistic thoughts, represents a harmful and damaging phenomenon for all athletes' performance, including football players.

**OVERTRAINING:** Injured state of the athlete, who reveals a clear decrease in physical, technical, mental efficiency.

Overtraining can be more or less serious, as it can last a few days, up to weeks or months. The symptoms, visible or not, induce real decline at the psychological, physiological, and biochemical levels, but above all of performance.

The general and specific level of performance appears to be in short order and worsens in the same time as the decline of the capacity for concentration, attention, and learning.

Too many negatives are added that are ill suited to the athlete/player which are the low desire to train, or compete, lower self-esteem, increased resting heart rate, widespread muscle pain, insomnia, nausea, gastrointestinal complaints, sore headaches, technical disability, etc.

In short, training too little hurts, but training too much is the same.

# THE QUALITY OF EXERCISES/PRACTICES

Moving on, **training sessions and plans must be structured with an educational aim** (technical, motor skills, and tactical). Therefore, we now talk about the quality of the exercise/practice, and not just the quantity.

Our attention moves first of all to **"Functional Circuits."**

All training plans should be based on the idea that the exercises/practices should activate specific "functional" motor patterns at the right balance between muscles and joints, as mentioned previously.

In regard to the exercises/practices to be proposed for the warm-up, there are **four areas to consider**:

1. Head, cervical tract, and thoracic tract of the vertebral column up to the fifth vertebra

2. Shoulder joint with shoulder blades, clavicles, and upper limbs

3. Thoracic and lumbar spine from the fifth to the twelfth vertebra included, lumbar region, pelvis, and hips

4. Lower part of the lumbar spine, hip joint, sacroiliac joint, and lower limbs

# UNOPPOSED, TECHNICAL OPPOSED, AND GLOBAL PRACTICES

# UNOPPOSED, TECHNICAL OPPOSED, AND GLOBAL PRACTICES

In classic scientific-sports literature, training practices are grouped into these three types.

- **Unopposed Practice:**
  The movements in the execution of the technical actions.

- **Technical Opposed Practice:**
  The technical actions with defensive resistance.

- **Global Practice:**
  The technical actions performed in a game-like situation.

So we go from the structuring of a technical action, of a skill, to using these techniques in a tactical context (individual or team).

Within these types of practice, these are the traditional sub-categories:

- **General Practices:**
  Aerobic, non-specific training, with or without the ball, mobilization, overload training, acrobatics, coordination, technique, running, jumping, speed, and strength, etc.

- **Special Practices:**
  Practice actions characteristic of situations in a football match but within a different organisation of time and space, rapid execution of technical actions, and motor skills, all within a technical-tactical practice.

- **Competitive Games:**
  Complete actions, with motor skills, technical actions, and movements like in a real match situation.

In regard to the method of conducting the activity, we opt for another classic subdivision:

- **Block Practice:**
  Sequence of exercises/practices where the same task is repeated several times.

- **Randomised Practice:**
  Sequence of exercises/practices in which a variety of different tasks are performed without a particular order - avoiding or minimising the consecutive repetitions of each task.

# Unopposed Practice Example

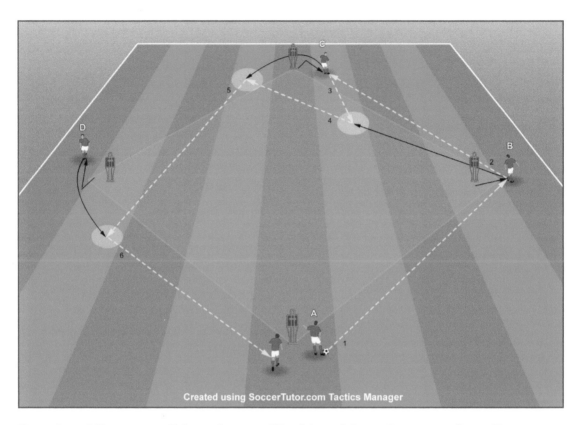

Created using SoccerTutor.com Tactics Manager

## Passing Warm-up Rhombus with Checking Away + One-Two

This passing warm-up practice does not include opponents, but the mannequins are there to represent them.

The players check away from the mannequins (defenders) and then move to receive the ball.

The receiving player creates the correct angle to receive, and the passer plays the pass at the correct time along the right shape (diagonal pass in rhombus).

It is a simple passing circuit with a one-two at Position C and a through pass for Player D's run.

The final pass from D is to the next player waiting at Position A (the start).

All players follow their pass around the circuit, so the player movement sequence is **A → B, B → C, C → D, D → A**

The aim of the practice is to warm up the players' bodies and simultaneously train the quality and precision of the technical actions.

**PASSING WARM-UPS**

# Technical Opposed Practice Example

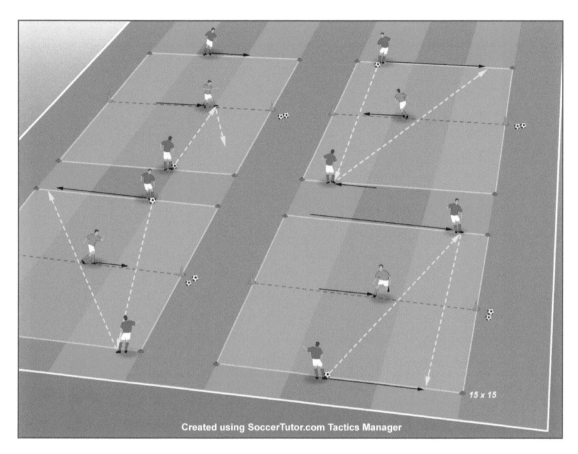

Created using SoccerTutor.com Tactics Manager

## Passing and Receiving Square with Middle Defender

This practice is in groups of 3 within a 15 yard square.

The 2 blue players are positioned outside at each end and the red player is positioned inside along the middle line, as shown.

The blue players have to pass the ball to each other without it being intercepted. The red defender can only move horizontally to try and intercept the ball.

You can either have a set amount of time for the defender in the middle, or have the players switch roles each time the ball is intercepted.

The aim of the practice is to warm up the players' bodies and simultaneously train the quality and precision of technical actions, while being aware of the presence of the opponent.

# Global Practice Example

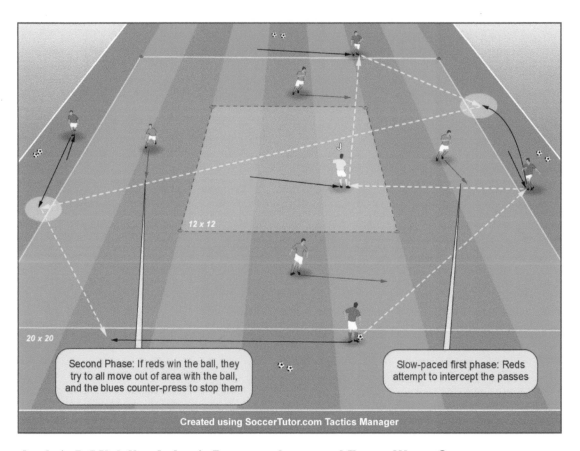

> **Second Phase:** If reds win the ball, they try to all move out of area with the ball, and the blues counter-press to stop them

> **Slow-paced first phase:** Reds attempt to intercept the passes

12 x 12

20 x 20

J

Created using SoccerTutor.com Tactics Manager

## 4v4 (+1 Middle Joker) Possession and Transition Game

As we progress to a "global practice," the players' involvement in the practice increases. The practice takes place in a 20 yard square with the 4 blue players outside on the sides. There is also a 12 yard square in the middle for the Joker.

In the **slow-paced first phase** (which is needed for the players to warm up properly), the 4 blue players keep possession of the ball, using the yellow Joker who can only move inside the smaller square. The red players try to win the ball but cannot enter the small

square. The blue and red players change positions after a set amount of time.

After a slow-paced first phase, the **second phase** adds an element - after the reds win the ball, they all move outside of the area and keep possession. The blues must counter-press to stop them.

The aim of the practice is to warm up the players' bodies and simultaneously train the quality and precision of technical actions, while competing against active opponents in a game-like situation.

# General Practice Example

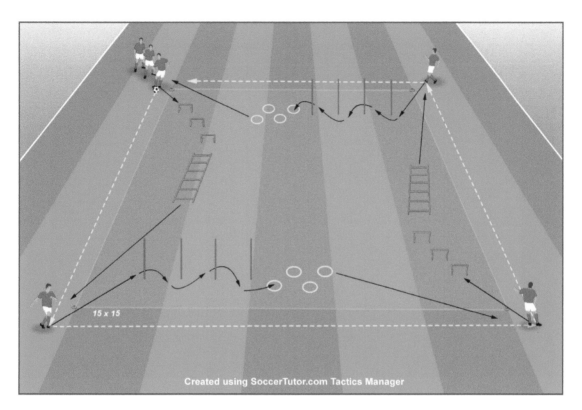

Created using SoccerTutor.com Tactics Manager

## Speed, Agility and Coordination Circuit in a Passing Square

With 5-8 players, we have 4 players starting outside each corner of the 15 yard square.

The ball is passed along the outside of the square to the next teammate, as shown.

After playing a pass, each player performs the speed and agility section in front of them.

They jump over the hurdles, slalom through the poles, take single leg steps through the speed rings, and use different steps through the ladders.

After finishing their section of the circuit, the players move to the next position and wait to receive a pass when the ball comes round again.

This warm-up practice is continuous.

# Special Practice Example

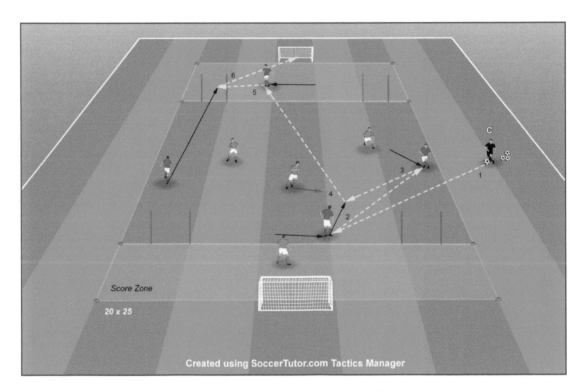

Created using SoccerTutor.com Tactics Manager

## Forward Support Runs Practice with Pole Gates, Target Man and End Scoring Zones

In a total area of 20 x 25 yards, we mark out 2 end "Score Zones" and position 4 pole gates and 2 small goals, as shown.

There is a 3 v 3 situation in the middle zone and each team has 1 player (attacker) in the scoring zone.

The coach starts the practice and the team in possession (blues in diagram) aim to direct the ball to the attacker.

The attacker receives within the end zone and passes (lay-off) for an oncoming teammate to score in the small goal.

The teammate who runs forward from the middle zone must do so through a pole gate and finish using only 1 touch.

The 3 defending players (reds) try to win the ball in the middle zone, and then quickly pass the ball to their attacker, who then passes (lay-off) for an oncoming teammate to score.

PASSING WARM-UPS

# Competitive Game Example

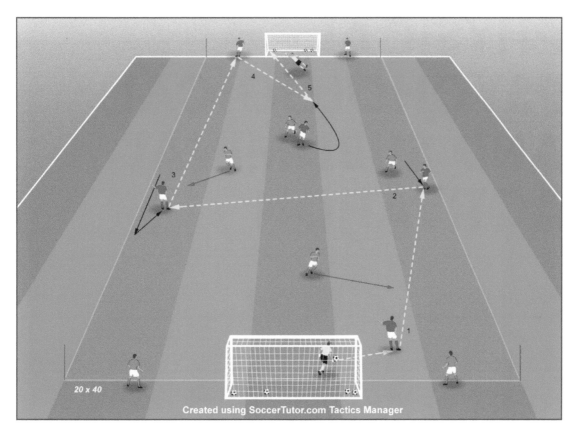

Created using SoccerTutor.com Tactics Manager

## 5(+2) v 5(+2) Dynamic Bounce Game with End Support Players

In a 20 x 40 yard area, each team has a GK and 4 outfield players inside.

On the outside end-line, each team has an additional 2 players as shown, who are limited to play to 1 touch.

The two teams play a normal game trying to score a goal. However, for a goal to be scored, it is only valid following a pass from an outside player.

Both sets of players must stay very alert. An attacking player must move quickly to receive back from the outside player (who only has 1 touch) in a position where they can shoot and score.

In addition, the defenders have to act quickly as soon as the ball is played to an opposing outside player, so they can track their opponents to stop them from receiving the bounce pass and scoring.

# PHYSICAL, PSYCHOLOGICAL, AND SUBLIMINAL ACTIVATION

*Editorial recognition: Vlad1998 / Shutterstock.com*

# "AWAKENING": BODY AND MIND ACTIVATION

When trying to apply scientific understanding in regard to football performance to the training pitch, a complex subject such as physiological psychology can provide a big helping hand.

**"Awakening"** quickly describes the process of excitement and waking up. It indicates the "load" and the "intensity" of the physiological and psychological warming up of the body.

Activation, psycho-physiologically speaking, is only the degree of activity of the nervous system.

From the state of sleep to awakening, the level of activation varies in a progressive way which we must keep in mind. Coaches must be able to make the players involved conscious.

Before a training session, the body prepares to face performance, moving from homeostasis to heterostasis, first of all alerting a series of well-defined processes:

1. **Immediate activation of the central nervous system** with increased ability for attention, concentration, and vigilance.

2. **Activation of the musculoskeletal system** with an increase in the ability of transmission, perception, and analysis of internal and external feedback.

3. **Activation of the sympathetic (automatic) nervous system** with consequent activation of the cardiovascular system

Research has been conducted over the years by physiologists and sports psychologists, aimed at highlighting the close connection between the activation we are dealing with and the performance, claiming that the "success," and the "result," may also depend on one "Light bulb that lights up or not."

The close relationship between the "light bulb that lights up and light that manages to emanate" was theorized by Yerkes and Dodson in 1908 with the representation of the trend as an **Inverted U**. This represents the relationship between the level of activation and performance. The theory is very simple to understand, and the graphic description is also easily "readable" and interpretable by everyone.

The **inverted symmetrical curve in the diagram** *(see the figure on the following page)* **shows the activation level** on the X axis and the level of performance on the Y axis.

With a **hyper-activation** level, the performance level is also low as shown. The player appears inattentive, and not very concentrated.

**PASSING WARM-UPS**

## Effect of Different Levels of Activation on Performance Levels

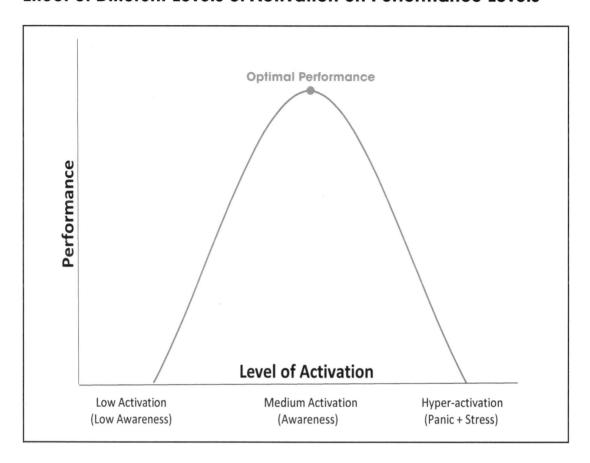

## What should a Coach do with this information about Activation and Performance levels?

The coach and coaching staff must be able to understand, through direct observation, objective evidence, tests, and medical analysis, if these sensations derive from physical fatigue, poor motivation, or from other causes.

If the activation increases from low to medium, the performance improves and arrives at maximum efficiency (calculable and comparable).

- See *Optimal Performance* on graph above, corresponding to the top of the inverted U.

**PASSING WARM-UPS**

# The "Flow State" - Playing at Full Commitment

This apex is defined by Yerkes and Dodson as the individual's **Flow State**, and it is the goal you must set yourself when you "manage" an athlete (football player) and schedule an individualised training session.

**FLOW STATE:** It was defined by the researcher Mihhali Csikszntmihalyi in the 1970s as a condition where the athlete in training loses the notion of everything he has around and cancels any distracting factors in favour of maximum mental concentration. It is a fusion between self and activity, a total immersion in commitment, faced only and exclusively for the pleasure of facing it.

In the flow state, **the body is overflowing with energy, all systems are at their maximum state** alert and all facilities are ready to express themselves best from a physical, motor, technical, tactical, and mental aspect.

Tangible positive symptoms are accelerations of the heartbeat without palpitations, increase in muscle tone, and absence of appetite.

Conditional, strength, speed and endurance, general and coordination capacities are free of inhibitory brakes.

A sprint is a true sprint (maximum speed), you run with the best possible explosive force, have the best possible ball trajectory reading ability, the best possible coordination for impact with the ball (e.g. A shot on goal), and in addition to all of this, it can also result in the best possible accuracy, power, etc.

Even the stress is adequate (**eustress - beneficial stress**), as the player is in full control of their actions, is boosted by a sense of well-being, self-esteem, mastery and belief in their capacity to execute actions and perform.

It is **the moment when concentration is maximal**, and there are no disturbing thoughts. The footballer is "loaded."

The role of the coach and of the coaching staff, is to extend the state of flow for as long as possible.

# The Dangers of Hyper-activation

If the activation rises higher and turns to **Hyper-activation**, the performance starts on the reverse path, and expires.

The technical actions and movements are affected by muscle tension and stiffness.

The quality in coordination is lost, sometimes abruptly, and less suddenly but equally significant, the fluidity of the motor actions/gestures.

Anxiety and stress curb cognitive abilities; concentration, attention, recognition of feedback, and the ability to solve problems diminish significantly.

Tangible negative symptoms, in this case, are increased sweating, decreased blood supply to the skin, tachycardia (high heart rate) with palpitations, tiredness, feeling of impossibility of recovery, facial tics, nausea, diarrhoea, and a possible urge to urinate repeatedly.

Poor control of emotional reactions begins to prevail (classic nervousness which can result in anger, and in yellow and red cards), tremors in the legs, fear of failure, and panic.

An excessive level of anxiety also causes a sharp and large release of **catecholamines** (hormones released into the body in response to physical or emotional stress) with a noticeable increase in blood sugar which, by consuming quickly, can make metabolic crisis and vasoconstriction at the muscle level with consequent reduction of blood supply and lactate toxicity.

The latter problem is very frequent in young players appearing for the first team without adequate physical and mental structures, and who are accused of not being "ready" and maybe "burnt out" after two performances. This is often due to a lack of knowledge/skills of those who should instead support them and guide them in the transition from the youth sector to the world of professional football.

**Too intense a warm-up can amplify the worst negatives of a performance in a match**.

We are, therefore, adamant to stay on the right side of the inverted U!
- *See figure on Page 38.*

# The Relationship Between Anxiety and Performance

Another particular theory concerning the relationship between anxiety and performance is that of Hanin, in the 1990s with insights following in the 2000s, which proposed the concept of **IZOF** *(see below)*.

The peculiarity of Hanin's theory lies in the fact that it does not consider positive or negative emotions that arise for the athlete during activities, as pleasant or unpleasant, welcome, or unwelcome, but only the functionality of the emotions themselves, in an orthodox and linear manner, that is if they are facilitating or debilitating.

## IZOF (Individual Zone of Optimal Functioning):

- **Individual -** The optimal operating zone is different for each athlete.

- **Zones -** The range of values is enlarged, and it cannot be defined or identified as a single value after which there is the immediate performance deadline.

- **Optimal Functioning -** The coaching staff manage peak performance by perfectly balancing the psycho-physical state with optimal conditions, and if the individual is a part of the "group" and has total involvement, they should have the appropriate and specific resources for the tasks to be performed to the optimum level.

The best preparation of a motor, technical, or tactical action, therefore, takes place on the medium activation level *(see figure on Page 38)*, when the "doses" of stress and anxiety are positive, driving, and stimulating.

If, on the other hand, the stresses have already done damage in the warming up phase, before the central part of the training session or of a competitive match, the performance will result in mediocre or bad play.

The stresses can be various and not always originated "by fault" of the coach. At youth level, the pressure of family members and/or poorly prepared managers, the climate, the unsuitable structures, may be the real cause of onset. This is the same for adult teams, plus a problem with one's partner, a bad relationship with the public, the importance of the match results for the continuation of the season, or even whether the salary is paid on time and in full.

The **responsibility of the coaching staff is to work out the right activation level that is fundamental to optimise the performance**. If anything it will be not identifying the problem and not having adapted to the warm-up exercise plans for one certain situation of activation, which changed over time and has not been taken into consideration due to laziness or incapacity.

# The Ideal "Curve" of Psychological Activation

Let us try to give an example, not clarifying entirely, but at least indicative of the ideal "curve" of psychological activation.

- **Low Level of Psychological Activation:**
  Preparing already known technical actions such as free kicks, corner kicks, or a goal kick the day before the match and morning of the match.

- **Medium (moderate) Level of Psychological Activation:**
  Preparing complex actions or decisive actions, such as a penalty kick, in the time period approaching the match. These types of activations are known by those who perform them, because an excessive state of excitement would compromise the optimum result!

- **A High Level of Psychological Activation:**
  This should always be avoided, but if it happens, try to transform it into positive energy, and a winning determination!

Obviously, the optimal awakening (activation) level is different for each of the players we deal with.

We must stress that performance level fluctuations are individual, and the coaching staff should "weigh" the corresponding awakening (activation) levels.

This job cannot be done by the coach or physical trainer alone, but may result from a cooperation between them, and/or better, between them and the sports psychologist, the only true and qualified figure of reference for these topics at a professional club.

It is difficult to organise a common warm-up for a group of football players who all have different psycho-psychological activation needs from each other.

However, you need to have the tools to analyse, devise and find suitable solutions to give the warm-up the role it needs. You need to make sure the main part of the training session (or the match) is where the players are at their optimum mental and physical levels.

You do not want to have the engine overheating before it has even left the garage!

# Managing Anxiety and Stress

There are classic **Breathing Exercises** that aim to control the breathing itself, adjusting the inhalation and exhalation phases to the intensity of the activities.

There are also **Meditation Exercises**, which originate from yoga, and these are the eight most popular meditation techniques:

- **Zen** (classic Buddhist sitting meditation)
- **Transcendental** (spiritual)
- **Vipassana** (visual and conscious meditation to provide "insight")
- **Mindfulness**
- **Ho'oponopono** (Hawaiian meditation for confession, repentance, and reconciliation)
- **Walking Meditation**
- **Kundalini** (moving energy through the body and releasing it)
- **Dynamic** (meditation with movement)

For **Visualisation Exercises**, rewarding moments can be used, such as a victorious match, goals scored, or a goal saving action. Alternatively, it can be a soothing vision, like imagining being on a sunny beach or green forest.

**"Emotional" Exercises** include describing good or great previous performances of yourself or others.

**Progressive Relaxation Techniques** such as that of Edmund Jacobson (conceived and experimented in the 1930s but illustrated and disclosed in 1959), is based on alternating the contraction and relaxation of specific muscle groups.

The **coaches need to manage the level of activation during the warm up**, and they will have to adapt aspects of the exercise/practice on the field of play, while it is going on.

The most common way is to **modify the rules of the practice**:

1. Add or remove competitive elements
2. Add or remove the possibility of point scoring/goals
3. Increase or decrease a time limit for which an action has to be completed
4. Reward for the winners
5. Penalty for the losers

The following is also important: The type of **communication and feedback used is another essential element**, modifying your tone of voice, the positive and negative feedback from one or more coaches positioned in different places on the field of play, and the optimal use of breaks and/or recovery phases.

# MOTOR IMAGERY AND SUBLIMINAL ACTIVATION

## THE ROLE OF "SPACE" IN FOOTBALL TRAINING

The size of the playing area is one of the fundamental parameters which must be analysed, studied, and understood by the coach. Then, through the right signals, to be transmitted to the players through the most suitable "geometric shapes," we can achieve the set goals.

It is clear that space, or spaces, during the various phases of the game, represent factors decisive for game situations, and for the technical and technical-tactical execution of game actions.

The next step is to understand that the representation of space is equally decisive, or the spaces that the football player's brain perceives and stores.

Space, as a concept, is what we can do "in and out" of it with and through our body, and with and through the various elements present (ball, teammates, opponents, goal). The appropriate interpretation of the continuous interweaving of relationships between these elements, therefore, determines the correct action and the success of the action itself.

The suitable motor behaviour (action), the correct technical action, and the exact tactical decision derive from the cognitive understanding of near-far, large-small, fast-slow, mobile-static, and are all dynamic and variable concepts.

## MOTOR IMAGERY

We must think in terms of the "idea" of action, and action as a priority for our brain.

It is known that there are populations of neurons called **canons**, which have the natural ability to take action both in response to a typical motor act, and to the visual stimulus connected to the motor stimulus in question.

Based on the **motor imagery** theory, recent studies have concluded that there is another type of population of neurons, called the **mirror**, which activate when a movement (or a technical action) must be made, and when there is vision of the same movement (or technical action) made by another individual (external visual feedback).

**Motor Imagery** is a subliminal activation, a feeling that remains below the perception threshold, but which still manages to influence the behaviour of the motor system. A typical life example for this would be the message from an advert on television.

Recent studies with **brain imaging techniques** such as **Functional Magnetic Resonance Imaging (fMRI)**

and **Transcranial Magnetic Stimulation (TMS)**, seem to indicate and confirm that mental imagination is also activated in the "primary" cortex source of the actual act.

The peculiar characteristic of mirror neurons is the "visual property." They are not activated by observing the objects with which there could be practical relationships, but instead observing acts and gestures performed by other individuals (instructions, demonstrations from coaches or other players).

When the visual feedback works, the football player becomes mentally predisposed (through mirror neurons) to perform actions the way they see them done. In this particular type of communication, the recipient develops a learning ability detail that "plays" on the visual-motor interaction produced by the action of the instructor (coach).

Through this complex system of return and conservation of images, the programmed motor movement of each individual is in continuous evolution, improving but also deteriorating if not guided by a well trained and aware coach.

Mirror neurons are neurons which are specialists of actions, so there are mirror neurons specialists for shooting on goal, mirror neurons specialists for dribbling, heading, etc.

Both canons and mirrors, continuously, by virtue of correct visual stimuli, can and must develop, expand, strengthen, and provide a kind of "vocabulary" of actions.

The more correct actions we will see, the more adjustments on the part of the coach there will be, the wider the possibility that our "vocabulary" improves in quality. The basis of success is the ability to decode visual messages, the production of "motor" words known and recognised as they have been decoded.

## THE ROLE OF THE COACH IN DEVELOPING PLAYERS

Responsibility for success must be equally distributed between the coach (teacher and transmitter) and the athlete (learner and receptor), whatever the level and whatever context you operate in.

The first form of motor learning (think of the small child who must learn to keep and use the spoon to eat the soup independently), is in fact **imitation**.

In football schools and youth academies, we are firmly convinced that a coach should know how to show a correct technical or motor action (a run, a pass, a shot, controlled touch, or a header) to hope to have a good and correct response from the students. However, this does not mean absolutely that he must necessarily have been a former professional footballer.

If a coach does not know how to best "demonstrate" something, the best strategy is to have it done by another coach or player. This is because all the players' mirror neurons are always alert and "lying in wait" to store the action and add it to their "vocabulary" for repetition.

# PERCEPTION

**Perception** is a "conscious and intentional process of the brain that allows the individual to select, recognise and integrate sensory information."

The information is transmitted to the spinal cord, then to the base of the brain and finally to the cerebral cortex.

Motor skills are preserved, however, at the subcortical level of the brain, in a safer and less breakable place than the one where the cognitive and verbal treasure is kept.

Tangible proof, such as who has learned to ride a bicycle or to ski as a child (complex skills), they will never forget it. While if we try to discuss the theory of Hegel's Idealism with our children because they learnt and "suffered" in High School, we would likely be disappointed.

*Editorial recognition: Vlad1998 / Shutterstock.com*

# TECHNICAL-TACTICAL WARM-UPS: TACTICAL PRINCIPLES AND SHAPES

*Editorial recognition: Vlad1998 / Shutterstock.com*

# WARM-UPS: USING DIFFERENT TACTICAL SHAPES

Taking a cue from geometry, a coach with clear ideas about the targets to pursue and achieve, must organise the warm-up exercises/practices in the correct space, depending on the number of players, their physical, technical, and tactical characteristics, and the environment in which they operate (ground, weather, etc).

The circle, triangle, rhombus, rectangle, hexagon, and the various combinations of these shapes, are an integral part of the planning and development of an integrated action, or series of complex actions.

## THE CIRCLE SHAPE

We do not believe the Circle has much value from a technical and tactical development aspect.

However, especially for warm-up practices, it creates the ideal environment for listening, being heard, observing, being observed, and for control.

It can also be beneficial for the coach to interpret the body language and messaging given off by the players without entering their individual space.

Within this intimate shape, unopposed practices in a circle including give and go, switching positions, etc, can highlight the sense of belonging to the group or not.

## THE RHOMBUS AND TRIANGLE SHAPES

On the other hand, the Rhombus is the simplest geometric shape to reproduce on the pitch and enables you to use the straight lines and points to create two triangles. The formation of triangles, the organisation of space and time, and the correct positioning of the triangles themselves speed up the development of the action and recognition of any variations.

The Triangle shape, unlike that of the circle, is also significant in the technical and tactical elements of football. Collaboration with three players, in the possession phase, for example, allows the optimisation of actions and synchronised movements, performed with precision, great dynamism, shrewdness and unpredictability. This is all for a better "tactical" management of the concepts of angles, penetration, positioning, defensive covering, etc.

## THE RHOMBUS, SQUARE, RECTANGLE, AND HEXAGON

The rhombus, the square, the rectangle, the hexagon, as "imagined spaces" reproduced in areas of the pitch increase the amount of possible passing lanes, the possibilities of technical and tactical choice for the player in possession of the ball, and of the players without the ball.

PASSING WARM-UPS

# WARM-UPS: TECHNICAL AND TACTICAL ELEMENTS

## TACTICAL WARM-UP ELEMENTS

Even during the warm-up phase of a training session, coaches must create the conditions to increase the number of ideas, expand and enhance the knowledge and skills of the individual, and the functionality of the collective (team). This should be for defence, midfield, and attack.

Specifically, we are convinced that the training plans within the geometrical shapes explained on the previous page, reinforce the links between the various players, and increase collaboration within a "tactical" criteria.

The players, even depending on the specific role and their tactical tasks, will consciously occupy precise positions, such as along the sides, in the corners, etc. Therefore, within the warm-up practice, they are reproducing countless possible game situations.

## TECHNICAL WARM-UP ELEMENTS

"Technical" elements with the ball such as passing, receiving, control, dribbling and one-two combinations will be combined with "Tactical" elements such as checking away from a marker, feints, shooting at goal, third man runs, crossing, support play, cutting runs, overlap runs, and defensive covering.

A brief explanation of the terms to be used to describe these elements is necessary. What the ball does and how the players move during the practices should be described.

Every technical and motor action represents the means by which the football player interacts with their environment:

1. **Acquiring the information** (perception-feedback)

2. **Analysing that information** (analysis and elaboration)

3. **Making the best decision for the situation** (formation of idea and putting it into action)

## VARIOUS TYPES OF PASS

**PASS:** A medium-distance pass to a teammate in space.

**THROUGH PASS:** Pass with strategic purposes, in behind the opposition's midfield (or defensive) line.

**CROSS:** The most targeted pass type for finishing on goal - low passed cross, high cross, from by-line or deep, to near post, far post, or centre of box.

**BACK-PASS:** A short-distance pass to a teammate usually positioned behind the line of the ball (in support).

**SUPPORT PLAY PASS:** A short-distance pass to the closest teammate to simply maintain possession, or to create space for the team to be able launch/finish an attack.

**LAY-OFF:** A short-distance pass used by the passer (attacker) to pass to an on oncoming teammate or set up a shot on goal for their teammate.

**LONG PASS:** Long pass to a teammate free in space who is able to open up the game (width or depth) and provide a genuine tactical development for the team.

**SWITCH OF PLAY:** Long pass to a teammate free in space - the tactical idea of expanding the game towards an area of the pitch where there are few opponents and plenty of space to exploit (opposition are vulnerable).

## RECEIVING AND BALL CONTROL

**DIRECTED CONTROL:** Taking a directional first touch when receiving a pass into space and into the same area you wish to then play.

It is a fundamental technical action in modern football, because pressing and pressure is now extremely intense.

Between the first touch (controlling the pass) and the next phase, there needs to be continuous action/movement. A directional first touch can be "open" or "closed" depending on the positioning of the opponent, the direction of the game and other game situation variables.

## MOVEMENTS WITHOUT THE BALL

**CUTTING RUN:** Diagonal movement of a player not in possession of the ball. This is done during an attacking action to "cut" diagonally across the opposition's defensive line and position yourself in a useful space to receive and control the ball.

**FORWARD RUN:** Forward movement of a player not in possession of the ball. The player makes a forward run into space (unmarked) and positions themselves to receive. Unlike cutting (diagonal) runs, forward runs are made with vertical movement.

**OVERLAP RUN:** Movement of a player (without the ball) on the outside of their teammate in possession, who can then pass forward and take their direct opponent out of the game.

# TECHNICAL-TACTICAL WARM-UPS: PRINCIPLES AND PRACTICES

## WARMING UP

We previously stressed that warming up is essential to activate the various functions of the body; to prepare the full body to a more physical, mental, and cognitive work capacity, and "prepare" the player for a chance to achieve optimum performance levels.

In addition, the warm-up allows the player to better manage heterostasis, a concept we have abundantly treated, to prevent injuries. Fatigue is an indicator for destabilised heterostasis, which is very dangerous *(see more detail on pages 14-15)*.

## TECHNICAL AND TACTICAL WARM-UP PRACTICES

A modern coach must know how to look beyond simply warming up the players.

The ultimate goal for all coaches is for their team to score one more goal than their opponents and win the game.

To be able to achieve this goal, the coach must know how to plan, propose, and apply their tactics.

These plans should be present during intelligent tactical-technical warm-up practices aimed at game development, and for the various stages of game development.

The knowledgeable coach will be able to break down and divide the various developments of the game to encourage the learning of both the individual game principles and the modifications through which players can collaborate successfully with each other.

It all starts with the "breakdown" of the game system into limited structures and the capacity of the players to recognise them and collaborate within the various geometric tactical shapes e.g. Rhombus, triangle, etc.

# THE RHOMBUS TACTICAL SHAPE

The rhombus is the geometric shape for football excellence. This **structure allows us to manoeuvre 360°** using the vertical plane (forward-backward and vice-versa) and the horizontal one (right-left and vice-versa).

The **positioning of the players is optimal and provides the player in possession with plenty of support**. The ball can be played from corner to corner.

The rhombus also makes cooperation between players easier, **facilitating combinations and exchanges**. The shape also **promotes mobility through positional changes** and organised and simplified management of spaces.

On the following pages, we are going to highlight some game related developments, focusing on the tactical rhombus shape, but also on the spaces that the tactical situation invites us to explore.

The team, as shown in the five tactical example diagrams to follow, are in the opponent's half and aim to pass to a free player in between the opposition's midfield and defensive lines.

From there, the hope is for the player who receives in between the lines to have the necessary time and space available to then make the correct decision and create a goal scoring opportunity.

Depending on the opposing defenders' positioning, movement and reactions, the free passing lanes, and the available spaces, the player in possession must be able to make the correct decision and follow up on this game development with perfect technical execution e.g. Final pass.

# RHOMBUS SHAPE - Tactical Example 1

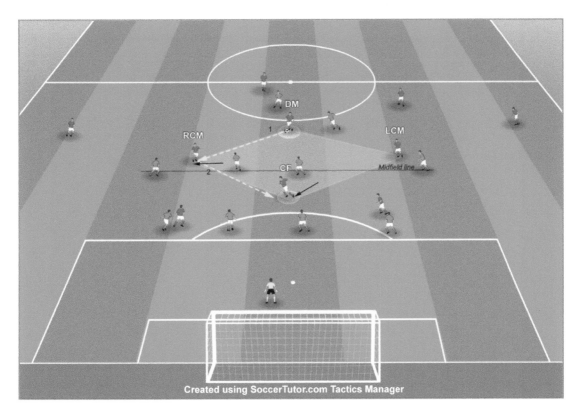

Created using SoccerTutor.com Tactics Manager

## Pass to the Advanced Player via the Wide Point of the Rhombus

The blue team have created a compact rhombus shape in the centre of the pitch with 4 players, as shown.

This example is based on the 4-3-3 but the team could be in different formations and still organise into this shape in possession e.g. 4-4-2, 4-2-3-1.

The defensive midfielder **(DM)** has the ball in the centre at the base of the rhombus. The primary aim is to pass to the centre forward **(CF)** at the advanced point of the rhombus shape in between the lines (unmarked).

The direct pass from the defensive midfielder **(DM)** to the centre forward **(CF)** is difficult to play in this situation, so the ball is passed to the player on the right side of the rhombus - right central midfielder **(RCM)**, and then to the most advanced player **(CF)**.

The centre forward **(CF)** receives unmarked with space to turn and attack in a 3v4 situation.

53

# RHOMBUS SHAPE - Tactical Example 2

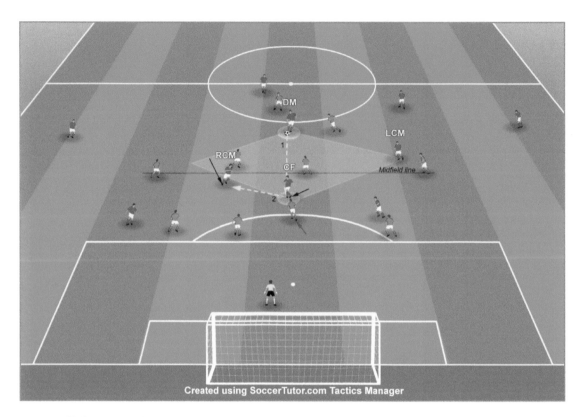

Created using SoccerTutor.com Tactics Manager

## Lay-off for the Forward Run of Central Midfielder when Pressed

In this second tactical example, the defensive midfielder **(DM)** again has the ball at the base of the rhombus shape in the centre of the pitch.

The aim is to pass to a player in between the lines (unmarked).

In this example, the defensive midfielder **(DM)** can pass directly to the player at the advanced point of the rhombus shape **(CF)**. However, the opposing red centre back is quick to move forward and prevent the centre forward from turning towards goal.

Therefore, the blue central midfielder **(RCM)** on the right side of the rhombus makes a forward run to receive the immediate lay-off pass.

The right central midfielder **(RCM)** receives between the lines facing the opponent's goal, with a promising 4v4 situation for the attack.

# RHOMBUS SHAPE - Tactical Example 3

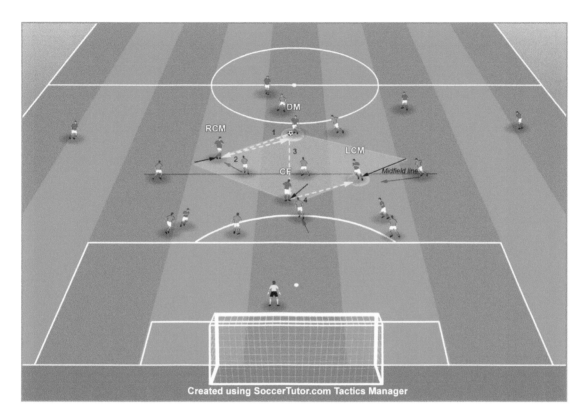

Created using SoccerTutor.com Tactics Manager

## One-Two, Forward Pass + Lay-off for Teammate when Pressed

In this third tactical example, the defensive midfielder **(DM)** again has the ball at the base of the rhombus shape in the centre of the pitch.

The aim is to pass to a player in between the lines (unmarked).

In this example, the defensive midfielder **(DM)** passes to the central midfielder **(RCM)** on the right of the rhombus, who is then pressed by the opposing red midfielder. Therefore, **RCM** plays back to the **DM**, completing a quick one-two combination.

The centre forward **(CF)**, at the top of the rhombus, moves across slightly to create a passing lane and receives the next pass from the defensive midfielder **(DM)**. The **CF** is then pressed by the opposing red centre back.

The blue central midfielder on the left side of the rhombus **(LCM)** makes a forward run to receive the lay-off pass.

The left central midfielder **(LCM)** receives between the lines facing the opponent's goal, with a promising 4v4 (+1) situation for the attack.

---

# RHOMBUS SHAPE - Tactical Example 4

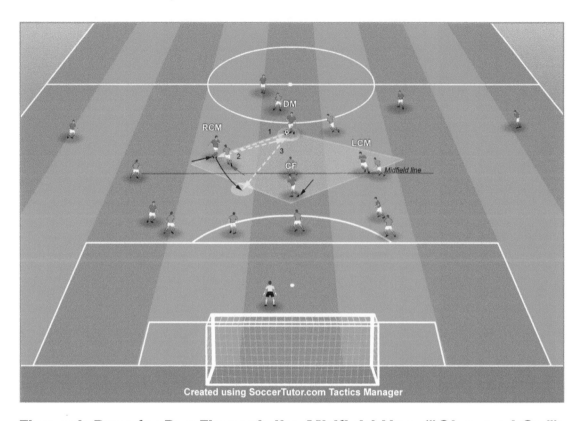

Created using SoccerTutor.com Tactics Manager

## Through Pass for Run Through the Midfield Line ("Give and Go")

This fourth tactical example is a variation of the previous one.

Again, the defensive midfielder - **DM** (base of rhombus) plays a quick one-two combination with the player on the right side of the rhombus **(RCM)**.

The right central midfielder **(RCM)** plays the ball back to the defensive midfielder **(DM)** because he is pressed by the red midfielder, and then makes a forward run to receive the next pass (third pass) in between the opposition's midfield and defensive lines.

The passing lane from the base of the rhombus (defensive midfielder - **DM**) to the player at the top of the rhombus (centre forward - **CF**) is not open.

The pass is played for the run of the right central midfielder **(RCM)**.

This completes a "give and go" for the **RCM** who receives between the lines facing the opponent's goal, with a promising 4v4 situation for the attack.

**PASSING WARM-UPS**

# RHOMBUS SHAPE - Tactical Example 5

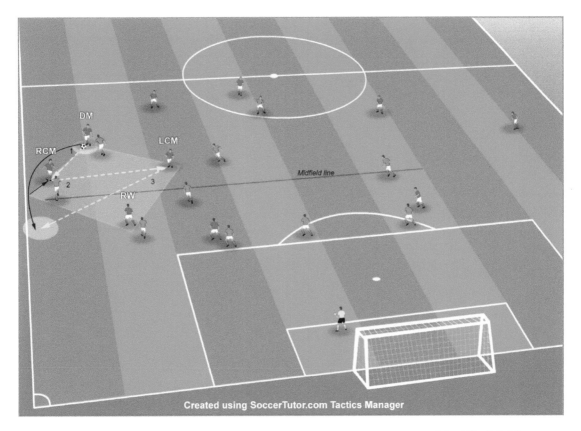

## Overlap Run from Base of Rhombus Through the Midfield Line

In this final tactical example using the rhombus, the shape is created out wide with the right winger **(RW)** at the top.

The player at the base of the rhombus **(DM)** passes to the **RCM**, who is pressed by a red midfielder. The **RCM** passes across to the player on the left side of the rhombus **(LCM)**.

As the player at the top of the rhombus **(RW)** is closely marked by the opposing red left back, the player at the base of the rhombus **(DM)** makes

an overlapping run around the **RCM**, which enables the easy diagonal pass from the **LCM** into the available space near the side-line.

After making an overlapping run, the defensive midfielder **(DM)** who was previously at the bottom of the rhombus, can receive and move forward into space with the ball.

There is now a 2v1 situation on the flank for the blue team's attack.

# THE TRIANGLE TACTICAL SHAPE

Another widely used geometric shape is the triangle. In this tactical situation, there are three players who collaborate and organise themselves within the triangular structure.

The ability to understand which spaces to direct the play is decisive to collectively manage the available spaces with good timing.

Again, we highlight game related developments, both using the triangle tactical shape, and the spaces that the tactical situation enables the team in possession to explore.

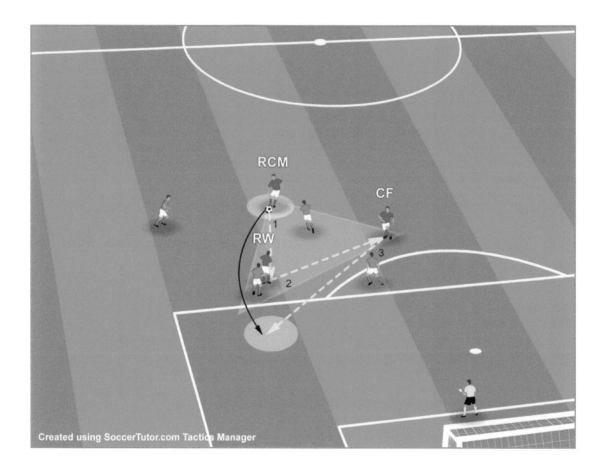

Created using SoccerTutor.com Tactics Manager

**PASSING WARM-UPS**

# TRIANGLE SHAPE - Tactical Example 1

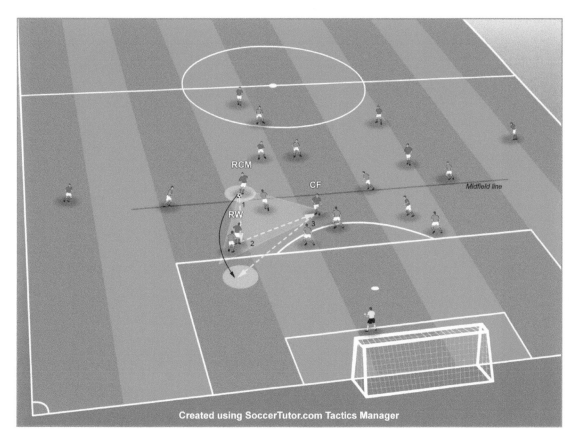

Created using SoccerTutor.com Tactics Manager

## Overlap Run from Base of Triangle in Behind Defensive Line

The blue team have created a triangle shape near the opposition's penalty box, as shown. This example is based on the 4-3-3 but the team could be in different formations.

In this first tactical example, the right central midfielder **(RCM)** has the ball at the bottom point of the triangle. The aim is to move the ball to a player in behind the opposition's defensive line.

The central midfielder **(RCM)** passes to the right winger **(RW)**, who is closely

marked from behind, so he passes across to the centre forward **(CF)**.

The central midfielder **(RCM)** makes an overlapping run outside the right winger **(RW)** to receive the centre forward's **(CF)** pass in behind the defensive line and inside the box, with a good opportunity to score.

This triangle passing pattern can be performed in various ways and in different areas of the pitch.

# TRIANGLE SHAPE - Tactical Example 2

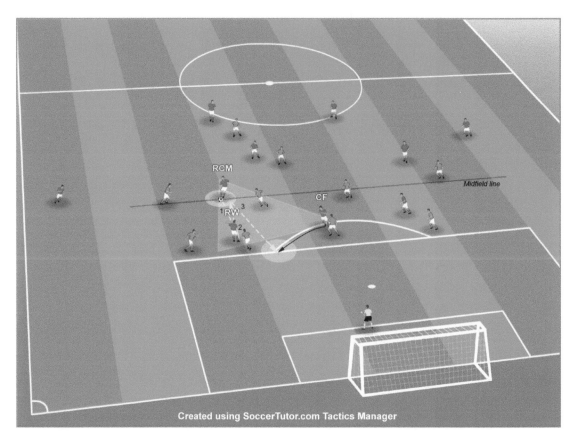

## One-Two + Third Man Run to Receive in Behind Defensive Line

In this second tactical example, the situation is slightly different.

After the right central midfielder's **(RCM)** pass from the base of the triangle to the right winger **(RW)**, the centre forward (**CF** - left side of triangle) is in a more advanced position and closer to his marker, therefore unable to receive the next pass.

The right winger **(RW)** instead passes back to the right central midfielder **(RCM)**, who is free to receive this time.

As soon as the ball is played back, the centre forward **(CF)** makes a well-timed curved run in between the two red centre backs and in behind.

The right central midfielder **(RCM)** plays a through pass for the run of the centre forward **(CF)**, who has a good opportunity to score in the box.

These triangle passing patterns can be performed in various ways and in different areas of the pitch.

# THE TACTICAL "Y SHAPE"

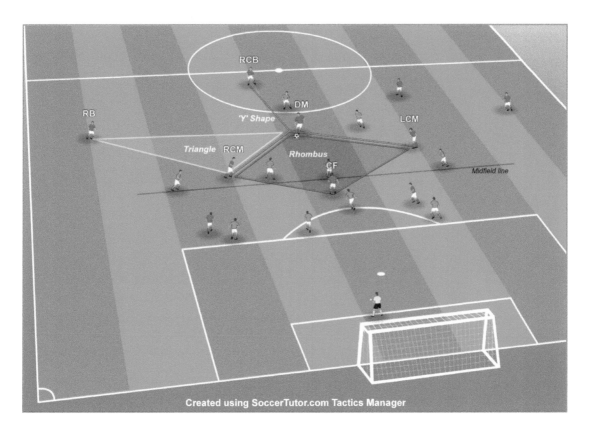

Created using SoccerTutor.com Tactics Manager

We now look at a typical team shape in possession of the ball using the 4-3-3 formation, which highlights the various geometric shapes that can be found. This example is based on the 4-3-3 but the team could be in different formations e.g. 4-4-2, 4-2-3-1, etc.

In this example, we have a **rhombus shape highlighted in blue** which includes the defensive midfielder **(DM)** at the base, the two central midfielders to the left **(LCM)** and right **(RCM)**, and the centre forward **(CF)** at the top.

A **triangle shape is highlighted in yellow**, which consists of the right back **(RB)**, the defensive midfielder **(DM)**, and the right central midfielder **(RCM)**.

The **"Y Shape" is highlighted by the red lines** and includes the right centre back **(RCB)** in the deepest position, the defensive midfielder **(DM)**, the left central midfielder **(LCM)**, and the right central midfielder **(RCM)**.

All of these shapes create passing lines to exploit for game development.

**PASSING WARM-UPS**

# TRAINING INDIVIDUAL TACTICAL PRINCIPLES: PLAYER MOVEMENT

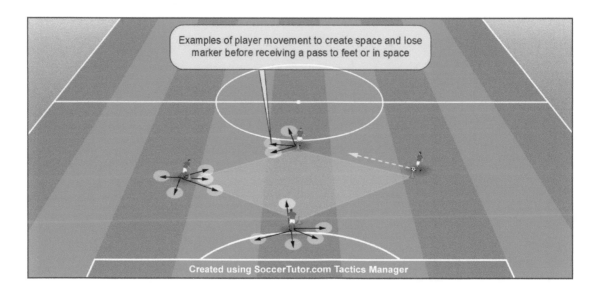

Examples of player movement to create space and lose marker before receiving a pass to feet or in space

Created using SoccerTutor.com Tactics Manager

We will highlight a series of simple passing practices used in professional training sessions, which have structures based on the geometric shapes we have talked about so far. But, before going into the comprehensive description and explanation of the practices, let us first understand the principles that players must know and recognise to be able to train at a higher level than just the technical execution.

As far as escaping a marker and creating space is concerned, it is possible to **train all the possible solutions for the players to play without the ball, in different positions**. The practice examples we show are all in the basic rhombus shape within the centre of the pitch, with one player in each corner.

The player at the base of the rhombus can move off the cone, open up, and move towards the ball to support the receiver.

The left and right players can open up to the side with respect to the cones, which represent opponents. They can move inside to receive or move to provide support, they can move forward, and move towards (to meet) the player in possession.

The player at the top of the rhombus can also come inside or towards the player in possession, move forward and in behind the opponent (cone), make a forward cutting run or open up to receive after moving forward.

The diagram above shows these options.

# COACHING LINK PLAY AND DECISION MAKING: PRACTICES

*Once the players have understood the "rules" with which to develop the different technical and tactical patterns/plans, it is then important that they are left free to connect with each other.*

*With examples, we want to try to explain the concept, highlighting the different developments that can arise from the choices of the players.*

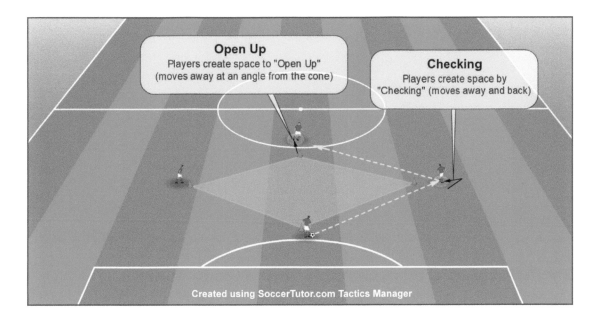

**Open Up**
Players create space to "Open Up" (moves away at an angle from the cone)

**Checking**
Players create space by "Checking" (moves away and back)

Created using SoccerTutor.com Tactics Manager

## SET-UP: Checking or "Open Up" to Create Space and Receive

In the diagram above, we show a simple set-up with four players in a rhombus shape. They pass to each other in an anti-clockwise direction, which can be reversed (clockwise) by the coach.

The first receiver makes their first movement "checking" away from the cone (represents opponent) and then makes their second movement back to receive the pass from their teammate.

The second receiver moves away at an angle from the cone (defender) and creates space to "open up." They can then take a good directional first touch and play an accurate well-weighted pass to the next player in the circuit.

From a tactical point of view, we can imagine a defensive midfielder, two central midfielders and a forward (or attacking midfielder).

# LINK PLAY & DECISION MAKING - Example 1

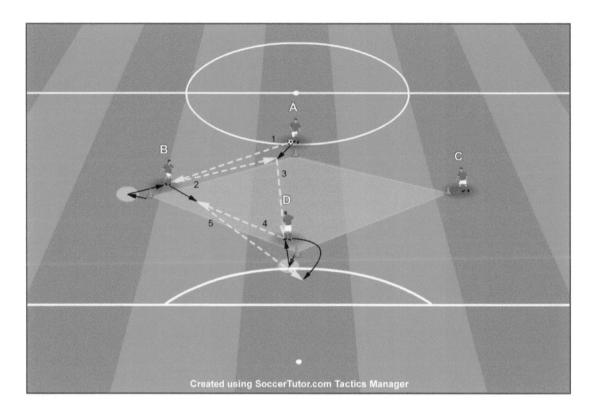

## One-Two, Forward Pass, Lay-Off + Final Pass in Behind

*On the previous page, we stressed the importance of leaving players free to connect with each other, and now we display two examples...* In this first practice example, we are working on link play and decision making in an anti-clockwise direction.

**Player A** starts the practice by playing a one-two combination with **Player B**. **Player B** has checked away from the cone and then moved towards his teammate to pass back. **Player A** moves to meet the return pass and passes to **Player D** (top of rhombus).

**Player D** checks away from the cone (defender) and then drops back to provide support and receive. He plays a lay-off pass back to **Player B**, who moves to meet the pass. **Player B** then plays a through pass for **D**, who spins in behind the cone (defender), as shown.

It is important to note the decisions of the receivers to occupy certain spaces instead of simply "opening up" and passing to the next player in the circuit. The practice then resumes in the opposite direction (clockwise) using **Player C**.

# LINK PLAY & DECISION MAKING - Example 2

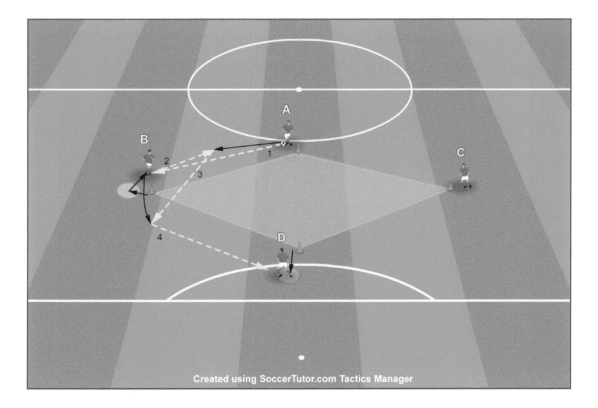

Created using SoccerTutor.com Tactics Manager

## One-Two, Through Pass + Diagonal Pass into Feet

In this variation of the previous example, **Player B** decides to check away from the cone and drop back to receive the first pass. **Player A** decides to move across towards his teammate to receive a short return pass.

**Player B** makes a run around the cone (forward) to receive **Player A's** through pass, and **Player D** moves forward off the cone to receive **Player B's** final pass with his back to goal.

From these examples, we show how you can give players the opportunity to express themselves freely. The game development changes depending on the choice of movement, whether the players open up to receive, move to inside to meet the pass, or drop back.

Depending on the decisions of the other players, the player at the top can decide to "come" for the ball or make a run in behind.

In these functional practices, the players work on tactical patterns but also on their technique, timing of movement, and decision making.

**PASSING WARM-UPS**

# THE DIRECTION OF PLAY

## Circuit Warm-up Practices

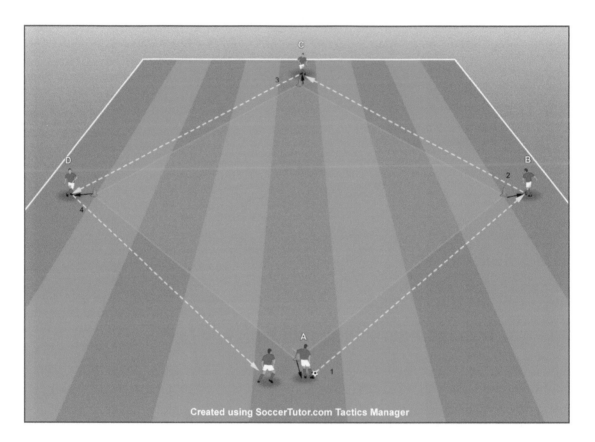

Created using SoccerTutor.com Tactics Manager

A final aspect to pay attention to is the direction of play.

There are **"Circuit Warm-ups"** (see diagram example above) which are not related to any specific game development, but aim to train aspects of individual tactics and pass and move combinations between a small group of players.

In the example above, the players simply pass around the rhombus (diamond) shape, and then follow their pass to the next position. More complex examples are shown later in the **Ancelotti** and **Guardiola** sections.

"Directional warm-ups" and "mixed warm-ups" examples are shown on the next two pages...

# Directional Warm-up Practices

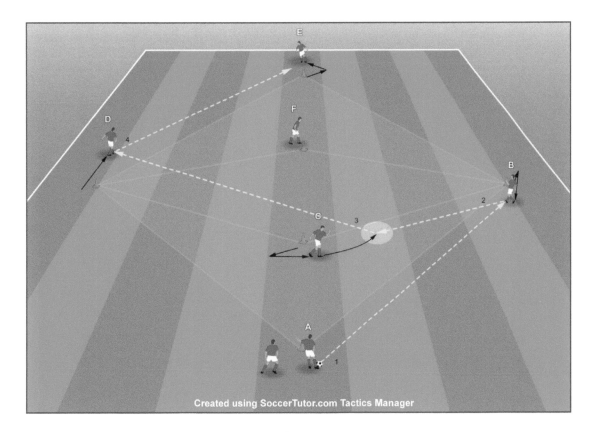

Created using SoccerTutor.com Tactics Manager

As you can see from the example above, **"Directional Warm-ups"** start from the bottom and the ball is moved to the top via a specific pattern of play sequence.

The pattern is then repeated in the opposite direction, repeating the same sequence as a mirror-image.

In the example above, **Player A** passes out wide to **Player B**, who checks away and drops back to receive. **Player B** then passes inside to **Player C**, who has checked away from the cone, and then moved across to meet the pass.

**Player C** plays a hard ground pass out wide to **Player D**, who moves forward off the cone to receive.

To complete the sequence, **D** passes to **Player E**. All players move to the next position (**A → B → C → D → E**).

The practice then restarts with **E's** pass to **Player D**, and the same pattern (mirrored) in the opposite direction.

You can see the best examples of directional warm-ups in the following **Carlo Ancelotti** section, and you can see an example of a "mixed warm-up" on the next page...

# Mixed Warm-up Practices

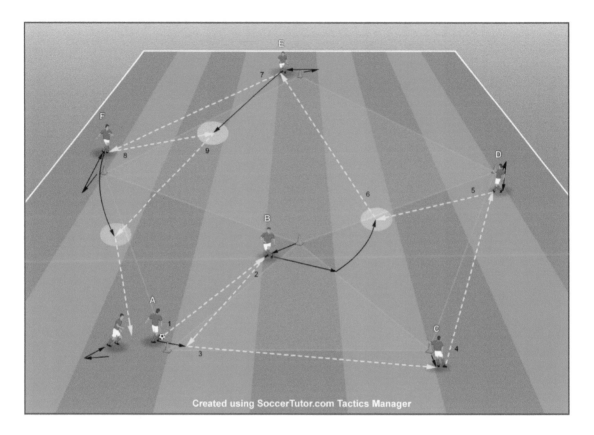

Created using SoccerTutor.com Tactics Manager

Finally, here is a **"Mixed Warm-up"** that combines the two aspects:

1. **Circuit warm-up**

2. **Directional warm-up**

Mixed warm-up practices work as a circuit, but also work with passing patterns from the bottom to the top and back, although the combinations do not have to be mirrored.

In the example above, **Player A** plays a one-two with **Player B**, who passes across to **Player C** - he passes forward to **Player D**, who is in a wide position.

**Player B** has moved across, and then moves forward to meet **D's** inside pass. **Player B** passes forward to **Player E**.

**Player E** plays a one-two with **F**, moves forward to receive the return, and plays a through pass for **Player F's** forward run around the cone. To complete the sequence, **Player F** passes to the start.

*The next section of the book shows warm-up practices observed directly from the training sessions of the following coaches: **Carlo Ancelotti**, **Pep Guardiola**, **Maurizio Sarri**, **Unai Emery**, **Diego Simeone** and **Jupp Heynckes**.*

68

# PASSING WARM-UPS DIRECT FROM THE WORLD'S TOP COACHES

**Carlo Ancelotti**

**Pep Guardiola**

**Diego Simeone**

**Unai Emery**

**Maurizio Sarri**

**Jupp Heynckes**

# DIAGRAM KEY

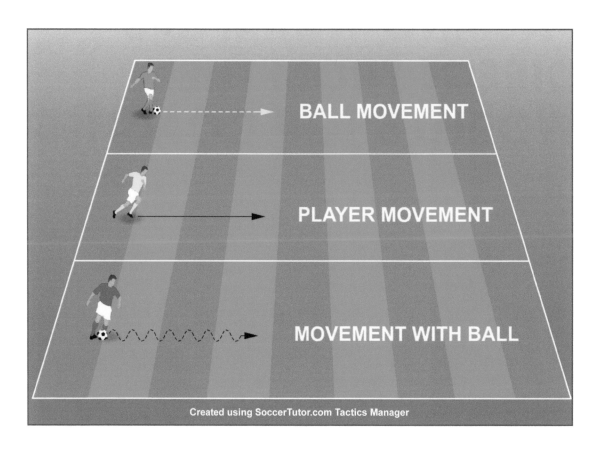

## PRACTICE FORMAT

### Each practice includes clear diagrams with supporting training notes such as:

- Name and objectives of practice
- Description of practice
- Variation (if applicable)
- Player movement sequence

# CARLO ANCELOTTI

## Technical-Tactical Passing Warm-ups

# CARLO ANCELOTTI: PROFILE

## COACHING ROLES

- **Real Madrid** (2021 - Present)
- **Everton** (2019-2021)
- **Napoli** (2018-2019)
- **Bayern Munich** (2016-2017)
- **Real Madrid** (2013 - 2015)
- **Paris Saint-Germain** (2011-2013)
- **Chelsea** (2009-2011)
- **AC Milan** (2001-2009)
- **Juventus** (1999-2001)
- **Parma** (1996-1998)
- **Reggiana** (1995-1996)

## HONOURS (Europe/World)

- **UEFA Champions League x 3** (2003, 2007, 2014)
- **FIFA Club World Cup x 2** (2007, 2014)
- **UEFA Super Cup x 3** (2003, 2007, 2014)
- **Intertoto Cup** (1999)

## HONOURS (Domestic Leagues)

- **German Bundesliga** (2017)
- **English Premier League** (2010)
- **Italian Serie A** (2004)

## HONOURS (Domestic Cups)

- **Spanish Copa del Rey** (2014)
- **English FA Cup** (2010)
- **Coppa Italia** (2003)
- **German DFL-Supercup x 2** (2016, 2017)
- **Supercoppa Italia** (2004)

## INDIVIDUAL AWARDS

- **European Coach of the Year—Alf Ramsey Award** (2003)
- **Globe Soccer Awards Best Coach of the Year** (2014)
- **IFFHS World's Best Club Coach x 2** (2007, 2014)
- **FourFourTwo 18th Greatest Manager of All Time** (2020)
- **Miguel Muñoz Trophy** (2015)
- **Ligue 1 Manager of the Year** (2013)
- **Serie A Coach of the Year x 2** (2001, 2004)

# 1. Basic Control, Pass and Move Rhombus Passing Circuit

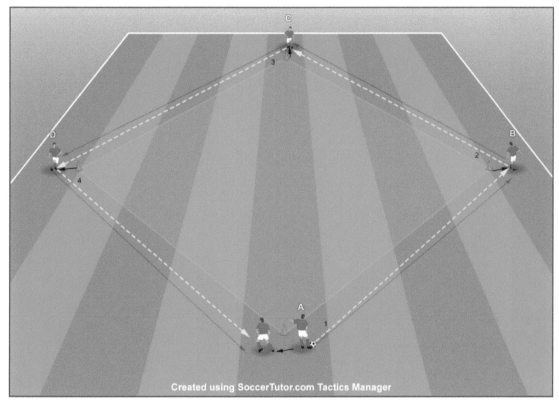

Created using SoccerTutor.com Tactics Manager

**General Objectives:** Passing and receiving within the key rhombus shape and using the correct body shape and control to prepare for the next action.

**Players:** 7-9 (2-4 extra players).

**Technical Objectives (1/2 touches):** Passing, receiving, body shape, and controlling the ball in the correct direction of the next action.

**Tactical Objectives:** Positioning and checking away (escaping marking to receive) at the correct time/angle.

**Description (10 yard rhombus):**

- A passes to B, who moves off the cone to receive.

- B passes to C, who does the same.

- C passes to D, who does the same.

- D passes to the next player waiting at the start position (A) and the practice continues.

- **Variation:** Reverse the direction.

- **Player Movement Sequence:**
  A → B, B → C, C → D, D → A.

---

**Source:** Carlo Ancelotti's Training Session with FC Bayern Munich (2016)

**PASSING WARM-UPS**

# 2. Dropping Back to Receive and Playing a "Give and Go"

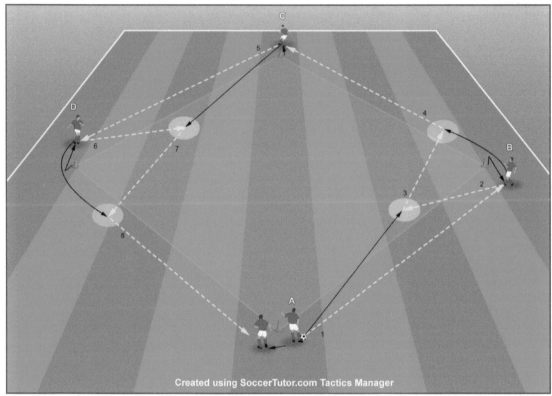

Created using SoccerTutor.com Tactics Manager

**General Objectives:** Passing and receiving within the key rhombus shape and using the correct body shape and control to prepare for the next action + one-twos.

**Players:** 7-9 (2-4 extra players).

**Technical Objectives (1/2 touches):** Passing, receiving, body shape, controlling the ball correctly to play the return pass and receiving on the move.

**Tactical Objectives:** Positioning, checking away (escape marker), and dropping back at the correct time/angle to receive.

**Description (10 yard rhombus):**

- A passes to B and then moves to provide support for the next pass. B checks away and drops back to receive, then passes to A (one-two) on the move.

- A passes for B to run onto around the cone to complete a "give and go."

- B passes to C. The same pattern is then repeated with Players C and D.

- D completes the sequence with a pass to the next player waiting at the start.

- **Player Movement Sequence:**
  A → B, B → C, C → D, D → A.

---

**Source:** Carlo Ancelotti's Training Session with FC Bayern Munich (2016)

# 3. Outside to Inside and Forward in a Rhombus Passing Circuit

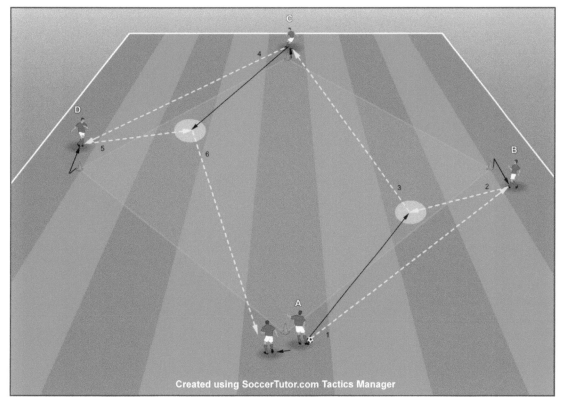

Created using SoccerTutor.com Tactics Manager

**General Objectives:** Passing and receiving within the key rhombus shape and using the correct body shape and control to prepare for the next action + support play.

**Players:** 7-9 (2-4 extra players).

**Technical Objectives (1/2 touches):** Passing, receiving, body shape, controlling the ball correctly to play the return pass, support play, and receiving on the move.

**Tactical Objectives:** Positioning, checking away (escape marker), and movement/ angles to provide support for teammates.

**Description (10 yard rhombus):**

- A passes to B and then moves to provide support for the next pass.

- B checks away and drops back to receive, then passes to A (one-two) on the move.

- A plays a hard ground pass to C, who opens up to receive. The same pattern is then repeated with Players C and D.

- D completes the sequence with a pass to the next player waiting at the start.

- **Player Movement Sequence:**
  A → B, B → C, C → D, D → A.

---

**Source:** Carlo Ancelotti's Training Session with FC Bayern Munich (2016)

**PASSING WARM-UPS**

# 4. One-Two Combinations and "Finding the Third Man Run"

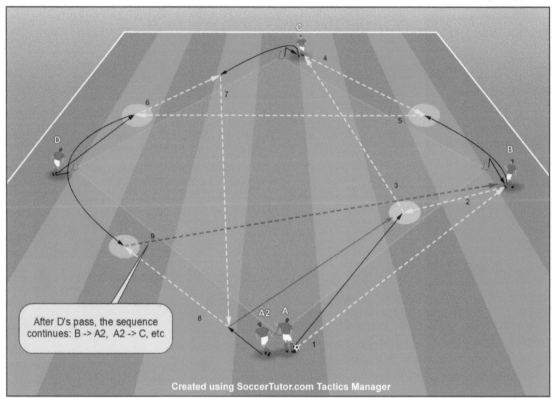

> After D's pass, the sequence continues: B -> A2, A2 -> C, etc

Created using SoccerTutor.com Tactics Manager

**General Objectives:** Passing and receiving within the key rhombus shape, support play, one-two combinations, forward movement to receive, and third man runs.

**Players:** 7-9 (2-4 extra players).

**Technical Objectives (1/2 touches):** Passing and receiving, body shape, controlling touch, support play, and through passes.

**Tactical Objectives:** Body shape, checking away (escape marker), positioning, support play, creating width, timing of forward movement, and finding the third man run.

**Description (10 yard rhombus):**

- A passes to B and then provides support.
- B passes back to A (one-two), who passes to C. Player B has moved forward (third man run) to receive back from C.
- B passes across to D and C moves to provide support.
- D passes back to C, who passes to the next player waiting at the start (A2).
- A2 passes for D to run onto and pass to B. The **sequence continues** with A2 moving to receive from B and passing to C, etc.
- **Movement:** A → B, B → C, C → D, D → A2.

Source: Carlo Ancelotti's Training Session with FC Bayern Munich (2017)

# 5. Progressing the Play - Receive with Back Foot, Control, and Pass

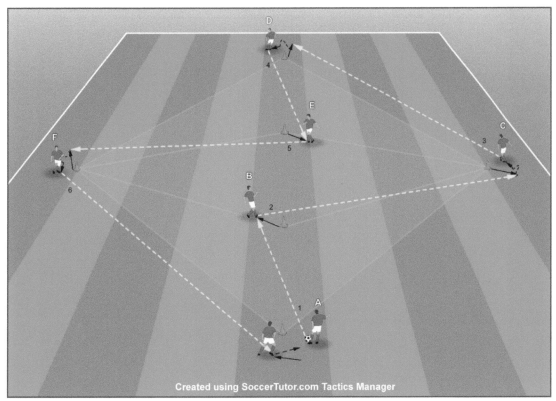

Created using SoccerTutor.com Tactics Manager

**General Objectives:** Progressing the play (full backs, midfielders and attacking midfielders), working on essential situational passing and receiving technical actions.

**Players:** 10-12 (3-5 extra players).

**Technical Objectives (1/2 touches):** Passing and receiving, checking away, and using the back foot to receive (directional first touch).

**Tactical Objectives:** Positioning, checking away, searching for width and depth to move the ball quickly and efficiently, creating width, and "angled" movements.

**Description (10 yard rhombus):**

- The passing sequence is as shown:
  A → B, B → C, C → D, D → E, E → F, F → A.

- All players move off their cone at an angle to receive + take a directional first touch in the direction of the next player/ pass.

- B and E move forward and to the side at an angle, C and F drop back at an angle, and D moves forward at an angle.

- **Player Movement Sequence:**
  A → B, B → C, C → D, D → E, E → F, F → A.

---

**Source:** Carlo Ancelotti's Training Session with FC Bayern Munich (2018)

**PASSING WARM-UPS**

# 6. "Outside to Inside" Movement to Receive, Control, and Pass

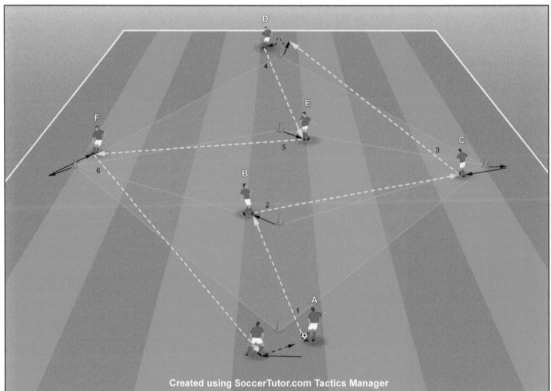

Created using SoccerTutor.com Tactics Manager

**General Objectives:** Progressing the play (full backs, midfielders and attacking midfielders), working on essential situational passing and receiving technical actions.

**Players:** 10-12 (3-5 extra players).

**Technical Objectives (1/2 touches):** Passing and receiving, checking away, moving inside to control with the outside of the foot.

**Tactical Objectives:** Positioning, "outside to inside" movement to create space (escaping markers) and receive on the move to progress the play quickly.

**Description (10 yard rhombus):**

- The passing sequence is as shown:
  A → B, B → C, C → D, D → E, E → F, F → A.

- C and F check away (outside) and then move inside to receive, take a directional controlling touch with the outside of the foot, and then pass.

- B, D, and E simply move off the cone at an angle, take a directional touch and pass.

- **Player Movement Sequence:**
  A → B, B → C, C → D, D → E, E → F, F → A.

---

**Source:** Carlo Ancelotti's Training Session with FC Bayern Munich (2018)

**PASSING WARM-UPS**

# 7. "Off the Ball" (Third Man Run) to Receive, Dribble, and Pass

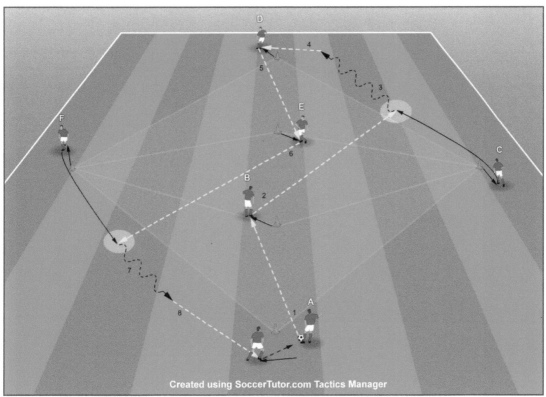

Created using SoccerTutor.com Tactics Manager

**General Objectives:** Progressing the play (full backs, midfielders and attacking midfielders), working on essential situational passing and receiving technical actions.

**Players:** 10-12 (3-5 extra players).

**Technical Objectives (1/2 touches):** Passing and receiving, timing runs off the ball, controlling the ball, and through passes.

**Tactical Objectives:** Positioning, checking away, utilising width and depth, passing forward to break lines, and off the ball movement with deep third man runs.

**Description (10 yard rhombus):**
- The passing sequence is as shown:
  A → B, B → C, C → D, D → E, E → F, F → A.
- C and F drop back (check away), and time runs forward to receive the next pass on the move. They then run forward with the ball before playing the next pass.
- B and E move off the cone at an angle to receive and play a diagonal pass, timed well for their teammate's run.
- **Player Movement Sequence:**
  A → B, B → C, C → D, D → E, E → F, F → A.

**Source:** Carlo Ancelotti's Training Session with FC Bayern Munich (2016)

# 8. Progressing the Play Using Inside Support with "Give and Go"

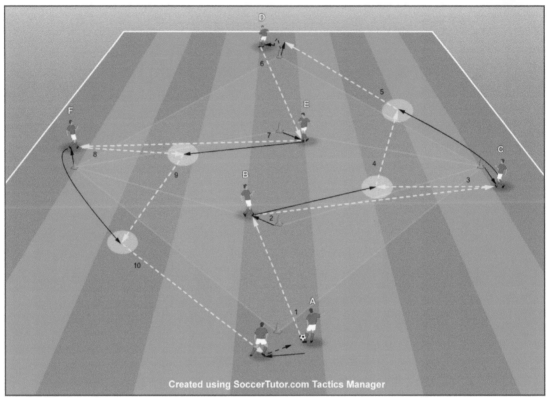

Created using SoccerTutor.com Tactics Manager

**General Objectives:** Progressing the play (full backs, midfielders and attacking midfielders), working on essential situational technical actions including "give and go."

**Players:** 10-12 (3-5 extra players).

**Technical Objectives (1/2 touches):** Pass and receive, "give and go," support play, timing runs off the ball, and through passes.

**Tactical Objectives:** Positioning, utilising width and depth, passing forward to break lines, forward runs, ability to read game situations, play in tight areas (give and go).

**Description (10 yard rhombus):**

- A passes to B, who passes to C. C passes inside for B, who moves across.

- B passes forward for the overlap run of C around the cone (give and go).

- C times his run well and passes to D.

- The same passing sequence is repeated on the other side (mirrored) in the opposite direction with D, E, and F.

- F passes to the next player waiting (position A) and the practice continues.

- **Player Movement Sequence:** A → B, B → C, C → D, D → E, E → F, F → A.

---

**Source:** Carlo Ancelotti's Training Session with FC Bayern Munich (2016)

# 9. Progressing the Play Using Inside Support and Forward Pass

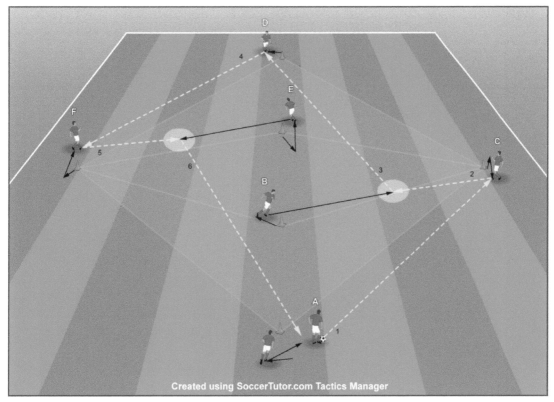

Created using SoccerTutor.com Tactics Manager

**General Objectives:** Progressing the play forward with the use of inside support play (full backs, midfielders and attacking midfielders).

**Players:** 10-12 (3-5 extra players).

**Technical Objectives (1/2 touches):** Pass and receive, support play, timing of movement, through passes, and accurate passing.

**Tactical Objectives:** Body shape, positioning, checking away (escape marker), utilising width and depth, read game situations, support play, and incisive forward passing.

**Description (10 yard rhombus):**

- A passes wide to C, who checks away and drops back to receive.

- C passes inside for the movement of B, who has checked off the cone and moved across to support. B then plays a hard diagonal ground pass to D.

- The same sequence is repeated on the other side (mirrored) with D, F, and E.

- E passes to the next player waiting (position A) and the practice continues.

- **Player Movement Sequence:**
  A → B, B → C, C → D, D → E, E → F, F → A.

**Source:** Carlo Ancelotti's Training Session with FC Bayern Munich (2018)

# 10. Continuous "Give and Go" Support Play Circuit

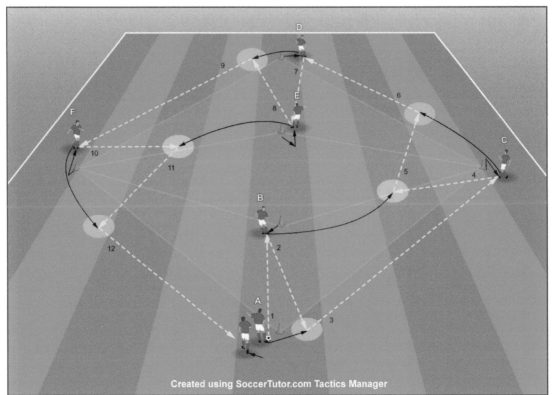

Created using SoccerTutor.com Tactics Manager

**General Objectives:** Combination play between the full backs and midfielders, and close exchanges (one-two combinations).

**Players:** 10-12 (3-5 extra players).

**Technical Objectives (1/2 touches):** Pass and receive, support play, timing of movement, through passes, one-twos, give and go.

**Tactical Objectives:** Positioning, checking away (escape marker), utilising width and depth, support play, passing forward to break lines, forward runs, reading game situations, and playing in tight areas (give and go).

**Description (10 yard rhombus):**

- A plays a one-two with B and passes wide to C. C passes inside for the movement of B, who moves across to support.

- B passes forward for the overlap run of C around the cone (give and go). C times his run well and passes to D.

- D plays a give and go with E and passes to F. F then plays a give and go with E.

- F passes to the next player waiting and the passing practice continues.

- **Player Movement Sequence:**
  A → B, B → C, C → D, D → E, E → F, F → A.

**Source:** Carlo Ancelotti's Training Session with FC Bayern Munich (2016)

# PEP GUARDIOLA

## Technical-Tactical Passing Warm-ups

**PASSING WARM-UPS**

# PEP GUARDIOLA: PROFILE

## COACHING ROLES

- **Manchester City** (2016 - Present)
- **Bayern Munich** (2013 - 2016)
- **Barcelona** (2008 - 2012)
- **Barcelona B** (2007 - 2008)

## HONOURS (Europe/World)

- **UEFA Champions League x 2** (2009, 2011)
- **UEFA Champions League Runner-up** (2021)
- **FIFA Club World Cup x 3** (2009, 2011, 2013)
- **UEFA Super Cup x 3** (2009, 2011, 2013)

## HONOURS (Domestic Leagues)

- **English Premier League x 3** (2018, 2019, 2021)
- **German Bundesliga x 3** (2014, 2015, 2016)
- **Spanish La Liga Primera División x 3** (2009, 2010, 2011)
- **Spanish Tercera (2nd) División** (2008)

## HONOURS (Domestic Cups)

- **English FA Cup** (2019)
- **German DFB-Pokal x 2** (2014, 2016)
- **Spanish Copa del Rey x 2** (2009, 2012)
- **English EFL Cup x 3** (2018, 2019, 2021)

## INDIVIDUAL AWARDS

- **FIFA World Coach of the Year** (2011)
- **Globe Soccer Awards Coach of Century** (2020)
- **European Coach of Season - Press Association** (2011)
- **European Coach of Year - Alf Ramsey Award** (2009)
- **English Premier League Manager of Season x 2** (2018, 2021)
- **LMA Manager of the Year x 2** (2018, 2021)
- **La Liga Coach of the Year x 4** (2009, 2010, 2011, 2012)

# 1. Support Play with One-Twos and Timing of Movement to Receive

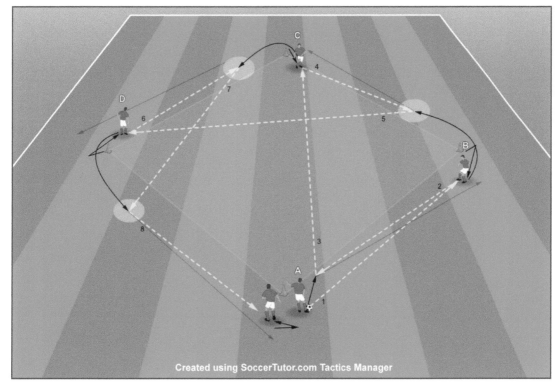

Created using SoccerTutor.com Tactics Manager

**General Objectives:** Passing and receiving (control), checking away (escape markers), and good timing of off the ball movement to create a micro-game situation.

**Players:** 7-9 (2-4 extra players).

**Technical Objectives (1/2 touches):** Passing and receiving with various types of passes; short, long, support, and through passes.

**Tactical Objectives:** Body shape, checking away (escape marker), game development (width and depth), support play, incisive movement, at game speed and intensity.

**Description (10 yard rhombus):**

- A plays a one-two with B, who checks away (off cone) and drops to receive.

- A passes to C, who lays the ball off for the run (around the cone) of B.

- B passes across to D, who lays the ball off for the run (around the cone) of C.

- C plays a through pass to D, who runs around the cone to receive. D passes to the next player waiting at the start position (A) - the practice continues.

- **Player Movement Sequence:**
  A → B, B → C, C → D, D → A.

---

**Source:** Pep Guardiola's Training Session with FC Bayern Munich (2015)

# 2. One-Twos, Timing of Movement + Through Pass for Third Man Run

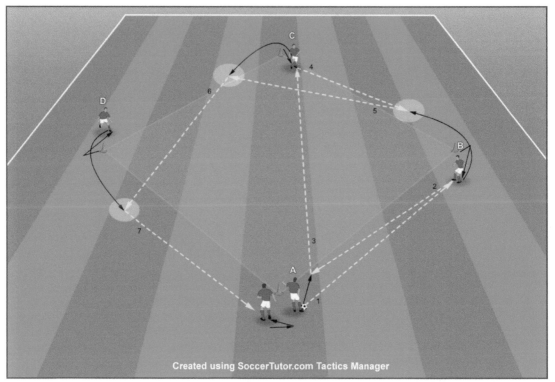

Created using SoccerTutor.com Tactics Manager

**General Objectives:** Passing and receiving (control), checking away (escape markers), and good timing of off the ball movement to create a micro-game situation.

**Players:** 7-9 (2-4 extra players).

**Technical Objectives (1/2 touches):** Passing and receiving with various types of passes; short, long, support, and through passes.

**Tactical Objectives:** Body shape, checking away (escape marker), game development (width and depth), support play, incisive movement, at game speed and intensity.

**Description (10 yard rhombus):**

- A plays a one-two with B, who checks away (off cone) and drops to receive.

- A passes to C, who lays the ball off for the run (around the cone) of B.

- B makes a well-timed pass for the run of C around the cone.

- C plays a through pass to D, who has dropped back and then run forward to receive. To finish, D passes to the next player waiting at the start position (A).

- **Player Movement Sequence:**
  A → B, B → C, C → D, D → A.

**Source:** Pep Guardiola's Training Session with FC Bayern Munich (2015)

# 3. Movement to Receive on the Run, with Dribbling and Through Pass

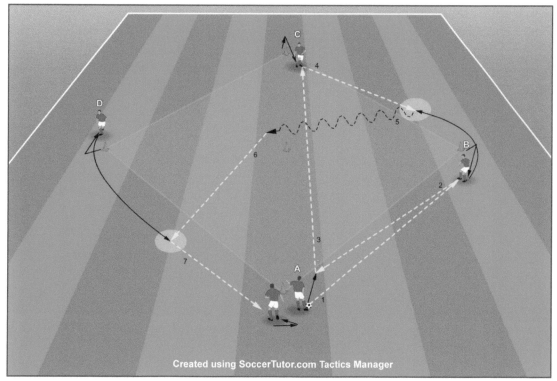

Created using SoccerTutor.com Tactics Manager

**General Objective:** Passing and receiving (step and control), first touch, checking away to escape markers, incisive movement without the ball, creating a micro-game situation.

**Players:** 7-9 (2-4 extra players).

**Technical Objectives (1/2 touches):** Checking away to receive, receiving, various types of passes; short, long, support, and through passes.

**Tactical Objectives:** Body shape, checking away (escape marker), game development (width and depth), support play, incisive movement, at game speed and intensity.

**Description (10 yard rhombus):**
- A plays a one-two with B, who checks away (off cone) and drops to receive.
- A passes to C, who lays the ball off for the run (around the cone) of B.
- B then dribbles inside and past the cone in the middle before passing into the path of D, who has checked away from the cone and then made a third man run (around the cone) to receive.
- D passes to the next player waiting at the start, and the practice continues.
- **Player Movement Sequence:** A → B, B → C, C → D, D → A.

**Source:** Pep Guardiola's Training Session with FC Bayern Munich (2015)

# 4. Movement to Receive with Marker Behind in a Support Play Circuit

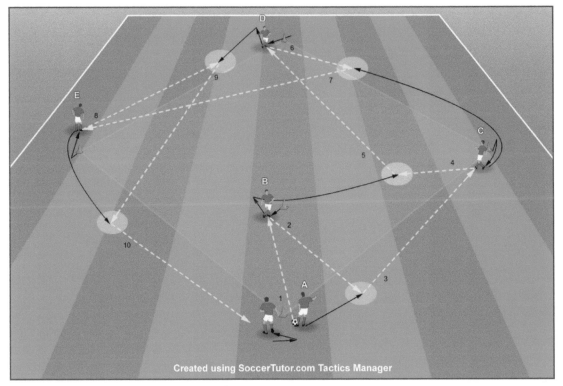

Created using SoccerTutor.com Tactics Manager

**General Objectives:** Creating space away from opponent behind, passing and receiving (directional control), and incisive movement in a micro-game situation.

**Players:** 8-10 (2-4 extra players).

**Technical Objectives (1/2 touches):** Passing and receiving with various types of passes; short, long, support, and through passes.

**Tactical Objectives:** Body shape, checking away (escape marker from behind), game development (width and depth), support play, incisive movement, at game speed and intensity.

**Description (10 yard rhombus):**

- A plays a one-two with B, moves across to meet the return, and passes wide to C.

- C plays inside for B, who moves across to meet the pass, then passes forward to D.

- D lays the ball off for C's run (around the cone), and C passes across to E.

- E lays the ball off for D, who then plays a through pass for the forward run of E.

- E had dropped back, and then run forward to receive. To finish, E passes to the next player waiting at the start.

- **Player Movement Sequence:**
  A → B, B → C, C → D, D → E, E → A.

---

**Source:** Pep Guardiola's Training Session with FC Bayern Munich (2015)

**88**

# 5. Support Play Circuit with Short, Long, Support and Through Pass

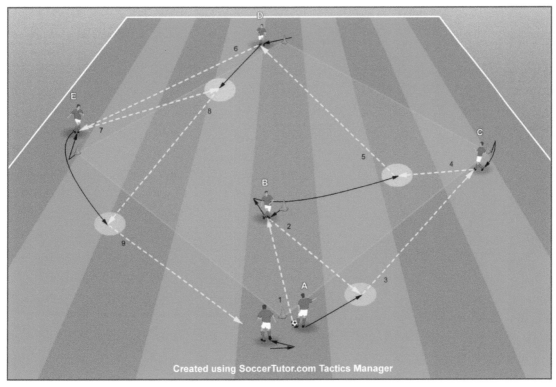

Created using SoccerTutor.com Tactics Manager

**General Objectives:** Creating space away from opponent behind, passing and receiving (directional control), and incisive movement in a micro-game situation.

**Players:** 8-10 (2-4 extra players).

**Technical Objectives (1/2 touches):** Passing, and receiving (with directional control), various types of passes; short, long, support, and through passes.

**Tactical Objectives:** Body shape, checking away (escape marker from behind), game development (width and depth), support play, incisive movement, at game speed and intensity.

**Description (10 yard rhombus):**

- A plays a one-two with B, moves across to meet the return, and passes wide to C.

- C plays inside for B, who moves forward, and then across to meet the pass. B passes forward to D.

- D plays a one-two with E, and then plays a through pass for E's forward run (overlap around the cone).

- E passes to the next player waiting at the start, and the practice continues.

- **Player Movement Sequence:**
  A → B, B → C, C → D, D → E, E → A.

**Source:** Pep Guardiola's Training Session with FC Bayern Munich (2015)

**PASSING WARM-UPS**

# 6. Movement to Receive, Support, Dribble, and Through Pass

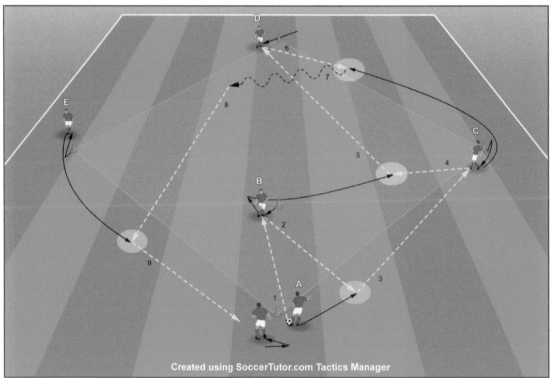

Created using SoccerTutor.com Tactics Manager

**General Objectives:** Creating space away from opponent behind, passing and receiving (directional control), and incisive movement in a micro-game situation.

**Players:** 8-10 (2-4 extra players).

**Technical Objectives (1/2 touches):** Passing, and receiving (with directional control), various types of passes; short, long, support, and through passes.

**Tactical Objectives:** Body shape, checking away (escape marker from behind), game development (width and depth), support play, incisive movement, at game speed and intensity.

**Description (10 yard rhombus):**

● A plays a one-two with B, moves across to meet the return, and passes wide to C.

● C plays inside for B, who moves forward, and then across to meet the pass. B passes forward to D.

● D lays the ball off for C's run (around the cone), and C dribbles across, as shown.

● C plays a through pass for the forward run (around the cone) of E.

● E passes to the next player waiting at the start, and the practice continues.

● **Player Movement Sequence:**
A → B, B → C, C → D, D → E, E → A.

**Source:** Pep Guardiola's Training Session with FC Bayern Munich (2015)

# 7. Complex Support Play Circuit with Rhombus + Triangle Shapes

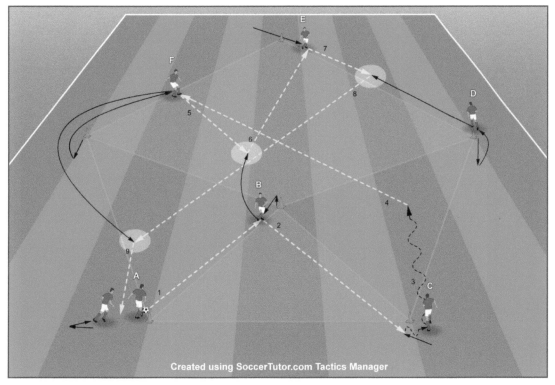

Created using SoccerTutor.com Tactics Manager

**General Objectives:** Creating space away from opponent behind, passing and receiving (directional control), and incisive movement in a micro-game situation.

**Players:** 10-12 (3-5 extra players).

**Technical Objectives (1/2 touches):** Checking away to receive, receiving, various types of passes; short, long, support, and through passes.

**Tactical Objectives:** Body shape, checking away (escape marker from behind), game development (width and depth), support play, incisive movement, at game speed and intensity.

**Description (8 Yard triangle / 10 yard rhombus):**

- A passes to B, and B to C, who moves inside, opens up, and dribbles forward.

- C passes diagonally to F, who had dropped back, and then made a forward run (around the cone) to receive.

- B spins to receive F's lay-off and passes to E, who makes a cutting movement. E lays the ball back for D's run, who then plays a long incisive through pass for the deep overlap run of F (around cone).

- F passes to the next player waiting.

- **Player Movement Sequence:**
  A → B, B → C, C → D, D → E, E → F, F → A.

---

**Source:** Pep Guardiola's Training Session with FC Bayern Munich (2015)

**PASSING WARM-UPS**

# 8. Complex Support Play Circuit with Through Pass to Third Man

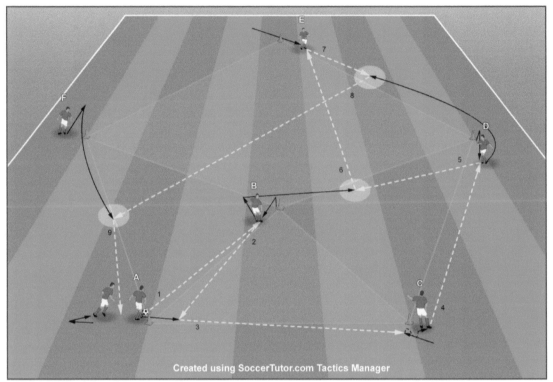

*Created using SoccerTutor.com Tactics Manager*

**General Objectives:** Creating space away from opponent behind, passing and receiving (directional control), and incisive movement in a micro-game situation.

**Players:** 10-12 (3-5 extra players).

**Technical Objectives (1/2 touches):** Checking away to receive, receiving, various types of passes; short, long, support, and through passes.

**Tactical Objectives:** Body shape, checking away (escape marker from behind), game development (width and depth), support play, incisive movement, at game speed and intensity.

**Description (8 Yard triangle / 10 yard rhombus):**

- A plays a one-two with B. A passes to C, who opens up and passes wide to D.

- B moves forward and then across to meet D's inside pass before passing forward to E.

- E lays the ball back for D's curved run around the cone.

- D plays a long diagonal through pass for the deep overlap run of F, who drops back before making the forward run.

- F passes to the next player waiting.

- **Player Movement Sequence:**
  A → B, B → C, C → D, D → E, E → F, F → A.

**Source:** Pep Guardiola's Training Session with FC Bayern Munich (2016)

# 9. Complex Support Play Circuit with "Give and Go"

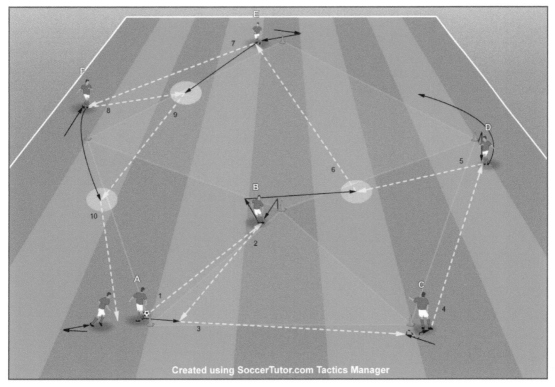

Created using SoccerTutor.com Tactics Manager

**General Objectives:** Creating space away from opponent behind, passing and receiving (directional control), and incisive movement in a micro-game situation.

**Players:** 10-12 (3-5 extra players).

**Technical Objectives (1/2 touches):** Passing, and receiving (directional control), checking away, various types of passes; short, long, support, and through passes.

**Tactical Objectives:** Body shape, checking away (escape marker from behind), game development (width and depth), support play, incisive movement, at game speed and intensity.

**Description (8 Yard triangle / 10 yard rhombus):**

- A plays a one-two with B. A passes to C, who opens up and passes wide to D.

- B moves forward and then across to meet D's inside pass before passing forward to E (who makes a double movement to create space and receive).

- E plays a one-two with F, and then plays a through pass for F's forward run (overlap around the cone).

- F passes to the next player waiting at the start, and the practice continues.

- **Player Movement Sequence:**
  A → B, B → C, C → D, D → E, E → F, F → A.

**Source:** Pep Guardiola's Training Session with FC Bayern Munich (2015)

# 10. Complex Support Play Circuit with Triangle Tactical Patterns

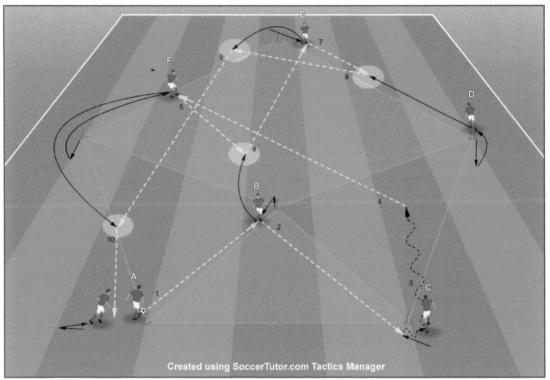

Created using SoccerTutor.com Tactics Manager

**General Objectives:** Creating space away from opponent behind, passing and receiving (directional control), and incisive movement in a micro-game situation.

**Players:** 10-12 (3-5 extra players).

**Technical Objectives (1/2 touches):** Passing, and receiving (directional control), checking away, various types of passes; short, long, support, and through passes.

**Tactical Objectives:** Body shape, checking away (escape marker from behind), game development (width and depth), support play, incisive movement, at game speed and intensity.

**Description (8 Yard triangle / 10 yard rhombus):**

- A passes to B, and B to C, who moves inside, opens up, and dribbles forward.

- C passes diagonally to F, who had dropped back, and then made a run (around the cone) to receive. B spins to receive F's lay-off and passes to E.

- E plays a "give and go" with D and receives after running around the cone.

- E plays a through pass for the deep curved overlap run of F (around cone), and F passes to the next player waiting.

- **Player Movement Sequence:**
  A → B, B → C, C → D, D → E, E → F, F → A.

**Source:** Pep Guardiola's Training Session with FC Bayern Munich (2015)

# MAURIZIO SARRI

## Technical-Tactical Passing Warm-ups

# MAURIZIO SARRI: PROFILE

## HONOURS

- **Italian Serie A** (2020)
- **UEFA Europa League** (2019)
- **Coppa Italia Serie D** (2003)

## INDIVIDUAL AWARDS

- **Serie A Coach of the Year** (2017)
- **Enzo Bearzot Award - "The Best Italian Manager of the Year"** (2017)
- **Panchina d'Oro - "Best Italian Association Football Coaches: Serie A"** (2016)

## COACHING ROLES

- **Lazio** (2021 - Present)
- **Juventus** (2019 - 2020)
- **Chelsea** (2018 - 2019)
- **Napoli** (2015 - 2016)
- **Empoli** (2012 - 2015)
- **Sorrento** (2011 - 2012)
- **Alessandria** (2010 - 2011)
- **Grosseto** (2010)
- **Perugia** (2008 - 2009)
- **Verona** (2008)
- **Various Clubs** (1990 - 2007)

# 1. Basic Passing and Receiving in a Tactical "Y Shape" Circuit

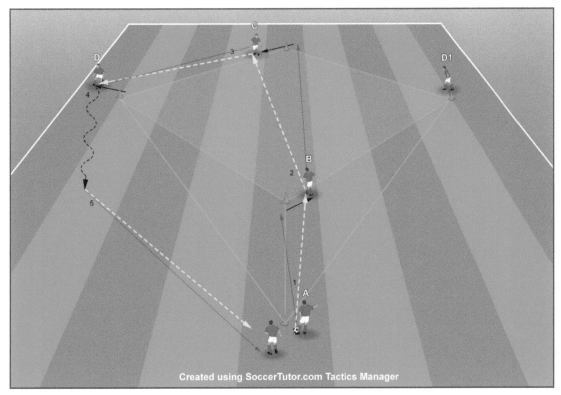

Created using SoccerTutor.com Tactics Manager

**General Objectives:** Basic passing and receiving technique, game development, timing of checking away and movements without the ball, and fast/synchronised play.

**Players:** 10-12 (4-6 extra players).

**Technical Objectives (1/2 touches):** Pass, receive, check away, directional touch, ball control, support play and through passing.

**Tactical Objectives:** Body shape, game development using width and depth, creating space to receive, and forming the rhombus and triangle shapes with two support options for the ball carrier.

**Description (10 yard distances):**

- A passes to B, who moves off the cone and opens up to receive.

- C moves to one side of the cone and B passes forward to him.

- C passes to D, who moves off the cone and opens up to receive.

- D runs with the ball and passes to the next player waiting (position A).

- The sequence is repeated using D1.

- **Player Movement Sequence:**
  A → B, B → C, C → D (or D1), D → A.

---

**Source:** Maurizio Sarri's Training Session with S.S.C. Napoli (2018)

# 2. Checking to Receive, One-Two and Through Pass for Deep Run

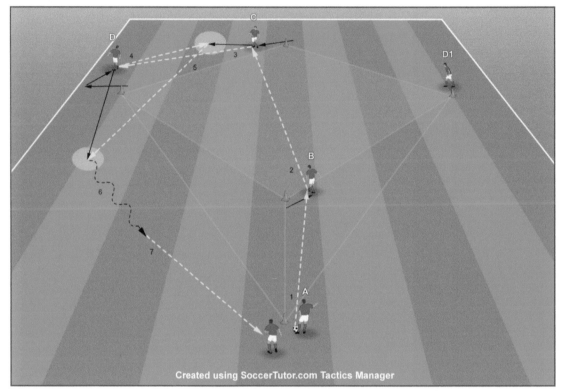

Created using SoccerTutor.com Tactics Manager

**General Objectives:** Game development and synchronised combination play to create "game timing" (accurate and correctly weighted passes for well-timed runs/movements).

**Players:** 10-12 (4-6 extra players).

**Technical Objectives (1/2 touches):** Pass, receive, check away, directional touch, ball control, support play, one-twos, give and go and through passing.

**Tactical Objectives:** Body shape, game development using width and depth, and creating space to receive (checking away).

**Description (10 yard distances):**

- A passes to B. C moves to one side of the cone and B passes forward to him.

- C plays a one-two with D, moving across to meet the return.

- D initially checks off cone, then moves to receive and play return pass to C. D then makes a third movement (opposite direction) to receive C's through pass.

- D runs with the ball and passes to the next player waiting (position A) - the same sequence is repeated using D1.

- **Player Movement Sequence:**
  A → B, B → C, C → D (or D1), D → A.

---

**Source:** Maurizio Sarri's Training Session with S.S.C. Napoli (2018)

# 3. Triple Movement to Check, Drop and Receive, and Make Overlap Run

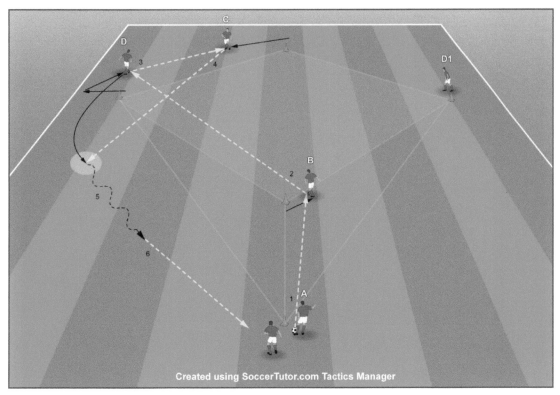

Created using SoccerTutor.com Tactics Manager

**General Objectives:** Game development, synchronised combination play, support play, timing of checking away and movements without the ball

**Players:** 10-12 (4-6 extra players).

**Technical Objectives (1/2 touches):** Pass, receive, check away, directional touch, ball control, support play, through passing and running with the ball.

**Tactical Objectives:** Body shape, game development using width and depth, creating space to receive (checking away) and support play.

**Description (10 yard distances):**

- A passes to B, who moves off the cone and opens up to receive.

- D checks and drops back to receive B's diagonal pass, then passes to C.

- C meets D's lay-off and plays a through pass for the third (opposite movement) of D on the overlap, for a give and go.

- D receives, runs with the ball, and passes to the next player waiting (position A) - the same sequence is repeated using D1.

- **Player Movement Sequence:**
  A → B, B → C, C → D (or D1), D → A.

**Source:** Maurizio Sarri's Training Session with S.S.C. Napoli (2018)

**PASSING WARM-UPS**

# 4. Forward Pass, Lay-off for "Give and Go" + Through Pass for Deep Run

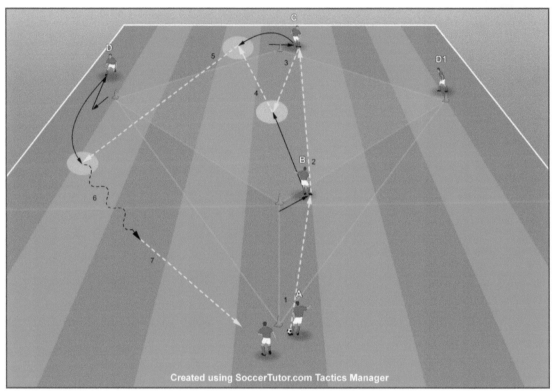

Created using SoccerTutor.com Tactics Manager

**General Objectives:** Synchronised combination play, timing of checking away and movements without the ball, fast combination play and incisive runs.

**Players:** 10-12 (4-6 extra players).

**Technical Objectives (1/2 touches):** Pass, receive, check away, directional touch, ball control, support play, through passing and running with the ball.

**Tactical Objectives:** Body shape, game development using width and depth, creating space to receive (checking away), support play, incisive runs, and overlaps.

**Description (10 yard distances):**

- A passes to B. C moves to one side of the cone and B passes forward to him.

- B moves to meet C's lay-off and passes back to him for C's run around the cone (to complete the give and go).

- D has initially made two movements. Finally, he makes a third (opposite) movement to receive C's through pass, run with the ball and pass to the next player waiting (A). The sequence is repeated using D1.

- **Player Movement Sequence:**
  A → B, B → C, C → D (or D1), D → A.

**Source:** Maurizio Sarri's Training Session with S.S.C. Napoli (2018)

**PASSING WARM-UPS**

# 5. Short Triangle Combination Play + Through Pass for Overlap (1)

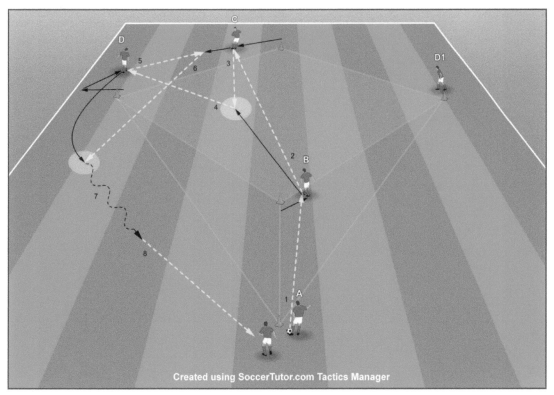

Created using SoccerTutor.com Tactics Manager

**General Objectives:** Synchronised combination play, timing of checking away and movements without the ball, fast combination play and incisive runs.

**Players:** 10-12 (4-6 extra players).

**Technical Objectives (1/2 touches):** Pass, receive, check away, directional touch, ball control, support play, through passing and running with the ball.

**Tactical Objectives:** Body shape, game development using width and depth, creating space to receive (checking away) and support play.

**Description (10 yard distances):**

- A passes to B. C moves to one side of the cone and B passes forward to him.

- B moves forward to receive C's lay-off. D checks and drops to receive the next pass from B.

- D plays a give and go with C, runs around the cone to receive the return pass on the overlap, and then runs with the ball.

- D passes to the next player waiting (A) and the sequence repeats using D1.

- **Player Movement Sequence:**
  A → B, B → C, C → D (or D1), D → A.

**Source:** Maurizio Sarri's Training Session with S.S.C. Napoli (2018)

**PASSING WARM-UPS**

# 6. Short Triangle Combination Play + Through Pass for Overlap (2)

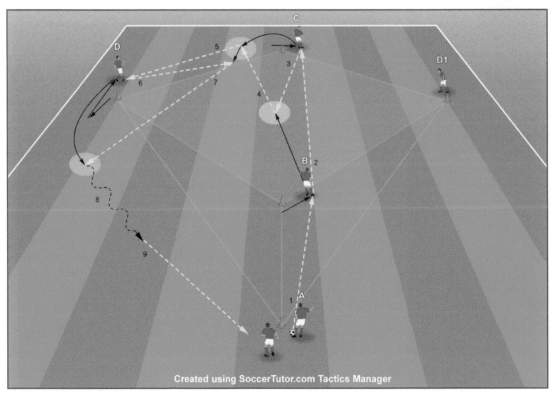

Created using SoccerTutor.com Tactics Manager

**General Objectives:** Synchronised combination play, timing of checking away and movements without the ball, fast combination play and incisive runs.

**Players:** 10-12 (4-6 extra players).

**Technical Objectives (1/2 touches):** Pass, receive, check away, directional touch, ball control, support play, through passing and running with the ball.

**Tactical Objectives:** Body shape, game development using width and depth, creating space to receive (checking away), support play, incisive runs, and overlaps.

**Description (10 yard distances):**

- A passes to B. C moves to one side of the cone and B passes forward to him.

- B moves to meet C's lay-off and passes back to him for C's run around the cone.

- D has checked, moved to receive the next pass from C, and then plays the return pass.

- C plays a through pass for D's third movement (opposite run). D receives, runs with the ball, and passes to the start - the sequence is repeated using D1.

- **Player Movement Sequence:**
  A → B, B → C, C → D (or D1), D → A.

**Source:** Maurizio Sarri's Training Session with S.S.C. Napoli (2018)

**PASSING WARM-UPS**

# 7. Forward Pass and Move to Support + "Give and Go" with Overlap

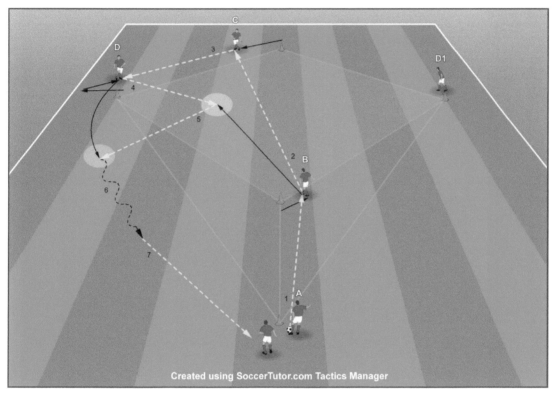

Created using SoccerTutor.com Tactics Manager

**General Objectives:** Synchronised combination play, timing of checking away and movements without the ball, fast combination play and incisive runs.

**Players:** 10-12 (4-6 extra players).

**Technical Objectives (1/2 touches):** Pass, receive, check away, directional touch, ball control, support play, through passing and running with the ball.

**Tactical Objectives:** Body shape, game development using width and depth, creating space to receive (checking away), support play, incisive runs, and overlaps.

**Description (10 yard distances):**

- A passes to B. C moves off the cone and B passes forward to him.

- C passes to D, who has checked and moved at an angle to receive. D passes for the forward run of B.

- B plays the return to complete the give and go for D's run around the cone.

- D receives, runs with the ball, and passes to the next player waiting (position A) - the sequence is repeated using D1.

- **Player Movement Sequence:** A → B, B → C, C → D (or D1), D → A.

**Source:** Maurizio Sarri's Training Session with S.S.C. Napoli (2018)

# 8. Deep Forward Pass + "Give and Go" within a Rhombus Shape

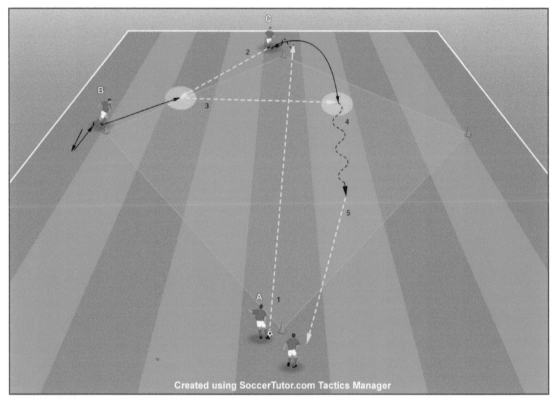

Created using SoccerTutor.com Tactics Manager

**General Objectives:** Timing of checking away and movements without the ball, and synchronised combination play.

**Players:** 6-8 (2-4 extra players).

**Technical Objectives (1/2 touches):** Pass, receive, check away, directional touch, ball control, support play, through passing and running with the ball.

**Tactical Objectives:** Body shape, game development using width and depth, creating space to receive (checking away) and support play.

**Description (10 yard rhombus):**

- A plays a hard ground pass to C, who opens up and takes a directional touch around the cone.

- B checks back and then moves forward and inside to meet C's lay-off pass.

- B then passes across the rhombus for the curved run of C around the cone.

- C receives, runs with the ball, and passes to the next player waiting (position A) - the same sequence is repeated.

- **Player Movement Sequence:**
  A → B, B → C, C → A.

**Source:** Maurizio Sarri's Training Session with S.S.C. Napoli (2018)

**PASSING WARM-UPS**

# 9. One-Two, Deep Forward Pass, Third Man Run, and "Give and Go"

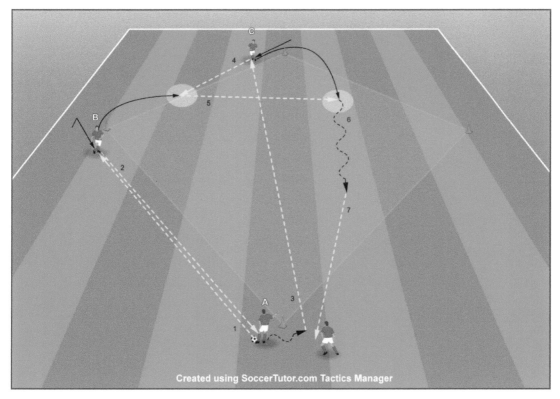

Created using SoccerTutor.com Tactics Manager

**General Objectives:** Timing of checking away and movements without the ball, and synchronised combination play.

**Players:** 6-8 (2-4 extra players).

**Technical Objectives (1/2 touches):** Pass, receive, check away, directional touch, ball control, support play, one-twos, give and go and through passing.

**Tactical Objectives:** Body shape, game development using width and depth, synchronised movement patterns, creating space to receive (checking away) and support play.

**Description (10 yard rhombus):**

- A plays a one-two with B, who drops back. A opens up to receive the return around the cone and passes to C, who moves off the cone to receive.

- B makes an opposite movement (curved run) around the cone to meet C's lay-off pass. B passes across the rhombus for the curved run of C around the cone.

- C receives, runs with the ball, and passes to the next player waiting (position A) - the same sequence is repeated.

- **Player Movement Sequence:**
  A → B, B → C, C → A.

**Source:** Maurizio Sarri's Training Session with S.S.C. Napoli (2018)

**PASSING WARM-UPS**

# 10. Three Player Combinations within a Double Triangle Structure

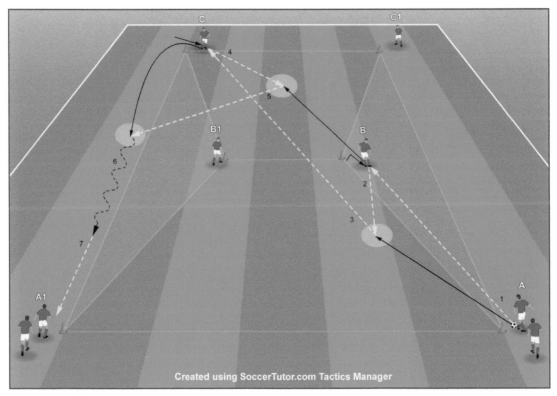

Created using SoccerTutor.com Tactics Manager

**General Objectives:** Tactical knowledge and implementation of game situation development in three player combinations.

**Players:** 10-12 (2-4 extra players).

**Technical Objectives (1/2 touches):** Pass, receive, check away, directional touch, ball control, support play, one-twos, give and go and through passing.

**Tactical Objectives:** Body shape, game development using width and depth, synchronised movement patterns, creating space to receive (checking away), support play and incisive runs.

**Description (10 yard distances):**

- A plays a one-two with B, moving forward at an angle to receive the return.
- A plays a hard diagonal ground pass to C, who moves off the cone.
- C passes back for the forward run of B.
- B plays the return pass to complete the give and go for C's run around the cone.
- C receives, runs with the ball, and passes to A1 - the same sequence is repeated (mirrored) with A1 → B1 → C1 → A.
- **Player Movement Sequence:** A → B, B → C, C → A.

**Source:** Maurizio Sarri's Training Session with S.S.C. Napoli (2018)

**PASSING WARM-UPS**

# UNAI EMERY

## Technical-Tactical Passing Warm-ups

# UNAI EMERY: PROFILE

## HONOURS (Europe)

- **UEFA Europa League x 4** (2014, 2015, 2016, 2021)

## HONOURS (Domestic Leagues)

- **French Ligue 1** (2018)

## HONOURS (Domestic Cups)

- **Coupe de France x 2** (2017, 2018)
- **Coupe de la Ligue x 2** (2017, 2018)
- **Trophée des Champions x 2** (2016, 2017)

## COACHING ROLES

- **Villarreal** (2020 - Present)
- **Arsenal** (2018-2019)
- **Paris Saint-Germain** (2016-2018)
- **Sevilla** (2013-2016)
- **Spartak Moscow** (2012)
- **Valencia** (2008-2012)

## INDIVIDUAL AWARDS

- **European Coach of the Season** (2014)
- **UNFP Manager of the Year** (2018)
- **Miguel Muñoz Trophy - Segunda División x 2** (2006, 2007)

# 1. Accurate Passing and Receiving in a Triangle Passing Circuit

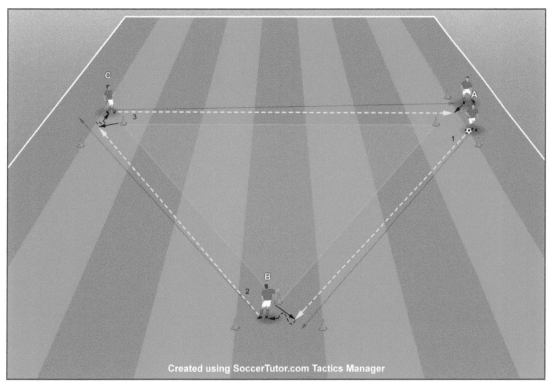

Created using SoccerTutor.com Tactics Manager

**General Objectives:** Passing and receiving within the key triangle shape, and oriented control for the next action.

**Players:** 6-8 players in each group (2 at each cone maximum + 2 extra).

**Technical Objectives (1/2 touches):** Precision passing (through cone gate), receiving, and directional control to prepare for the next action.

**Tactical Objectives:** Body shape, positioning, moving to create space to receive, and passing wide.

**Description (10 yard triangle):**

- A passes to B through the first cone gate and in front of the second gate.

- B moves off the cone to receive and takes a directional controlling first touch around the cone.

- The same is repeated with B and C, and C passes to the next player waiting. The same passing sequence is repeated.

- **Variation:** Reverse the direction.

- **Player Movement Sequence:** A → B, B → C, C → A.

---

**Source:** Unai Emery's Training Session with Sevilla FC (2013)

# 2. Directional Touch Through the Cone Gate + Beat the Defender

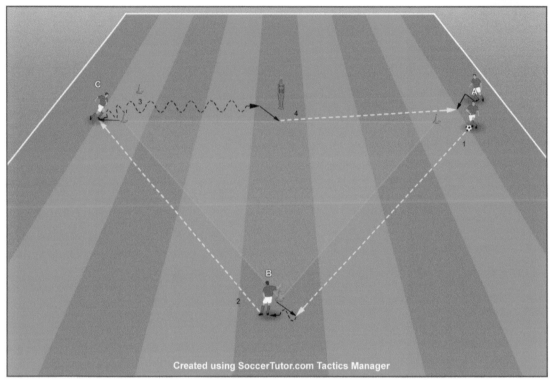

Created using SoccerTutor.com Tactics Manager

**General Objectives:** Passing and receiving within the key triangle shape, oriented control for the next action, improving control of the ball, ability to run with the ball, and feint/dribble.

**Players:** 6-8 players in each group (2 at each cone maximum + 2 extra).

**Technical Objectives (1/2 touches):** Precision passing (through cone gate), receiving, directional control to prepare for the next action, feints, and dribbling.

**Tactical Objectives:** Body shape, using angles, and beating the defender.

**Description (10 yard triangle):**

- A passes to B, who moves back off the cone to receive and passes to C.

- C takes a good directional first touch from behind the cone to move through the cone gate.

- C then runs with the ball up to the mannequin (defender) and performs a feint to dribble past it on either side.

- The sequence is completed with C's pass to the next player waiting (position A).

- **Player Movement Sequence:**
  A → B, B → C, C → A.

---

**Source:** Unai Emery's Training Session with Sevilla FC (2013)

**PASSING WARM-UPS**

# 3. Double One-Two, Dribbling, and Feint to Beat the Defender

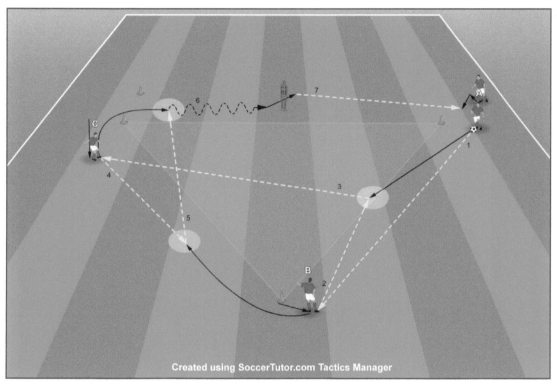

Created using SoccerTutor.com Tactics Manager

**General Objectives:** Passing and receiving within the key triangle shape, one-two combinations, improving control of the ball, dribbling, and feints.

**Players:** 6-8 players in each group (2 at each cone maximum + 2 extra).

**Technical Objectives (1/2 touches):** Passing and receiving, first touch (control) on the move, one-two combinations, support play, through passes, off the ball movement, timing runs, feints, and dribbling.

**Tactical Objectives:** Body shape, playing with width, support play, escaping marker.

**Description (10 yard triangle):**

- A passes to B, who plays back for A to run onto (one-two). A passes across to C, who drops back to receive. B runs around the cone to meet the next pass.

- C plays a give and go with B and times his curved run through the cone gate well to receive the return pass.

- C then runs with the ball up to the mannequin (defender), performs a feint to dribble past it and passes to the next player waiting (position A).

- **Player Movement Sequence:**
  A → B, B → C, C → A.

---

**Source:** Unai Emery's Training Session with Sevilla FC (2013)

# 4. Quick Combination, Through Pass, Check Away + Incisive Third Man Run

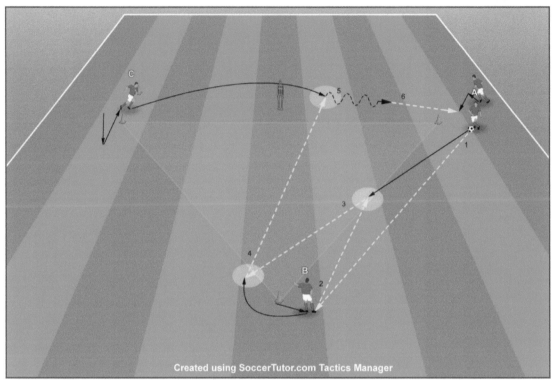

Created using SoccerTutor.com Tactics Manager

**General Objectives:** Passing and receiving within the key triangle shape, combination play, creating space, through passing, third man run, receiving on the move.

**Players:** 6-8 players in each group (2 at each cone maximum + 2 extra).

**Technical Objectives (1/2 touches):** Passing and receiving, first touch (control) on the move, one-two combinations, support play, through passes, ball control.

**Tactical Objectives:** Body shape, playing with width, support play, escaping marker (to receive), and third man run.

**Description (10 yard triangle):**

- A passes to B, who plays back for A to run forward onto (one-two).

- B moves around the cone to receive again, and A passes to him.

- C drops back first (checks away), then moves forward, and finally across past the mannequin, to receive B's pass.

- C controls the ball on the move, runs with the ball, and then passes to the next player waiting (position A).

- **Player Movement Sequence:**
  A → B, B → C, C → A.

---

**Source:** Unai Emery's Training Session with Sevilla FC (2013)

**PASSING WARM-UPS**

# 5. Close Combination Play and Incisive Pass + Receive on the Move

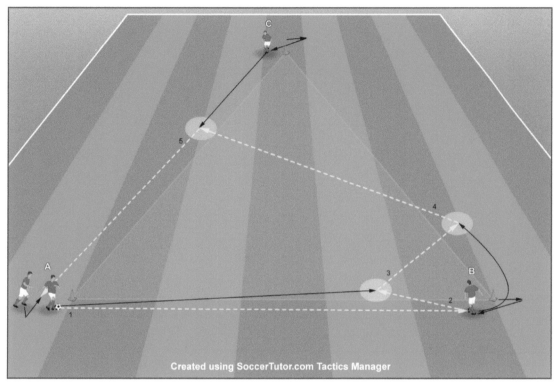

Created using SoccerTutor.com Tactics Manager

**General Objectives:** Passing and receiving within the key triangle shape, technical combination play, reading the game situation, incisive and well-timed play.

**Players:** 6-8 players in each group (2 at each cone maximum + 2 extra).

**Technical Objectives (1/2 touches):** Passing and receiving, first touch (control) on the move, one-two combinations, support play, and through passes.

**Tactical Objectives:** Body shape, playing in tight spaces, support play, escaping marker (to receive), and timing of run off the ball.

**Description (10 yard triangle):**

- A passes to B and follows his pass to provide immediate support.

- B plays a give and go with A, moving around the cone for the return pass.

- C checks away before timing his run well to receive B's pass across.

- C controls the ball on the move and passes to the next player waiting (position A) - the practice continues.

- **Player Movement Sequence:**
  A → B, B → C, C → A.

---

**Source:** Unai Emery's Training Session with Sevilla FC (2013)

**PASSING WARM-UPS**

# 6. Triangle Support Play with Double "Give and Go"

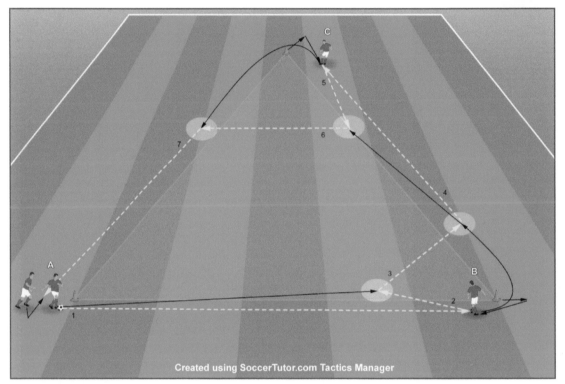

Created using SoccerTutor.com Tactics Manager

**General Objectives:** Passing and receiving within the key triangle shape, technical combination play, reading the game situation, incisive and well-timed play.

**Players:** 6-8 players in each group (2 at each cone maximum + 2 extra).

**Technical Objectives (1/2 touches):** Passing and receiving, one-two combinations, oriented control (directional first touches), and support play.

**Tactical Objectives:** Body shape, playing in tight spaces, short combinations, support play, and escaping markers (to receive).

**Description (10 yard triangle):**

- A passes to B and follows his pass to provide immediate support.

- B plays a give and go with A, moves around the cone for the return pass, and passes to C who drops back to receive.

- C plays a give and go with B, moving around the cone to receive the return.

- C takes a directional first touch on the move and passes to the next player waiting (position A).

- **Player Movement Sequence:**
  A → B, B → C, C → A.

**Source:** Unai Emery's Training Session with Sevilla FC (2013)

# 7. Triangle Support Play with Forward Pass and "Give and Go"

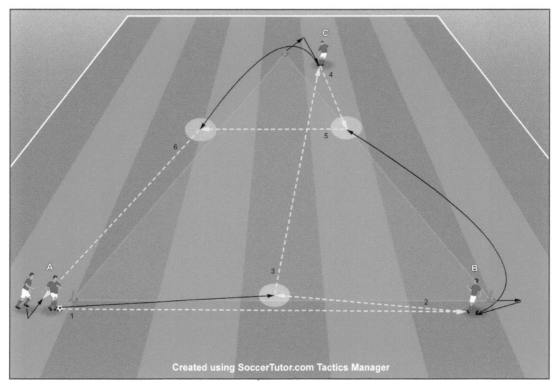

Created using SoccerTutor.com Tactics Manager

**General Objectives:** Developing players for different game situations using width (wide passes) and forward (through) passes.

**Players:** 6-8 players in each group (2 at each cone maximum + 2 extra).

**Technical Objectives (1/2 touches):** Passing and receiving, one-two combinations, oriented control (directional first touches), and support play.

**Tactical Objectives:** Body shape, escaping markers (to receive), synchronised combinations and movements, playing wide and forward, and support play.

**Description (10 yard triangle):**

- A passes to B and follows his pass to provide immediate support.

- B passes back for A and runs around the cone to support C.

- A passes to C, who plays a give and go with B, moving around the cone to receive the return pass.

- C takes a directional first touch on the move and passes to the next player waiting (position A).

- **Player Movement Sequence:**
  A → B, B → C, C → A.

---

**Source:** Unai Emery's Training Session with Sevilla FC (2013)

**PASSING WARM-UPS**

# 8. Triangle Support Play with Forward Pass and Lay-off

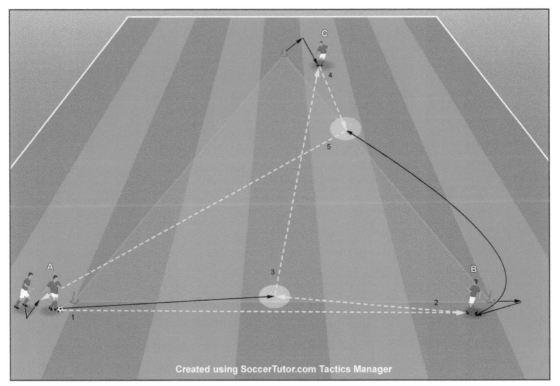

Created using SoccerTutor.com Tactics Manager

**General Objectives:** Passing and receiving within the key triangle shape, technical "sharp and fast" combination play, and reading the game situation.

**Players:** 6-8 players in each group (2 at each cone maximum + 2 extra).

**Technical Objectives (1/2 touches):** Passing and receiving, support play, through passes, first touch (control), and one-two combinations.

**Tactical Objectives:** Body shape, synchronised combinations and movements, playing wide and forward, support play, and unmarking movements.

**Description (10 yard triangle):**

- A passes to B and follows his pass to provide immediate support.

- B passes back for A and runs around the cone to support C.

- A passes to C, who lays the ball off for the run of B.

- B takes a directional first touch on the move and passes to the next player waiting (position A) - the practice continues.

- **Player Movement Sequence:** A → B, B → C, C → A.

**Source:** Unai Emery's Training Session with Sevilla FC (2013)

**PASSING WARM-UPS**

# 9. Triangle Support Play with Dummy + One-Two ("Give and Go")

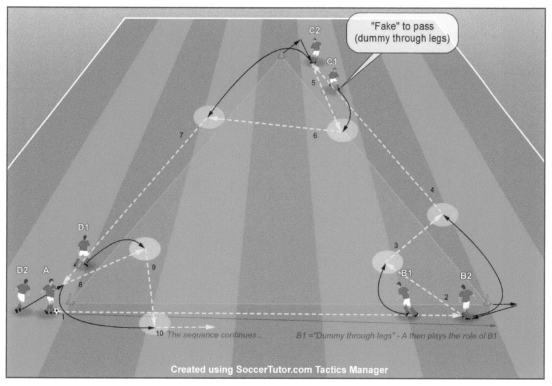

"Fake" to pass
(dummy through legs)

*The sequence continues...*     *B1 = "Dummy through legs" - A then plays the role of B1*

Created using SoccerTutor.com Tactics Manager

**General Objectives:** Passing and receiving within the key triangle shape, technical "sharp and fast" combination play in small space and reading the game situation.

**Players:** 9-10 (2-3 extra players).

**Technical Objectives (1/2 touches):** Passing and receiving, one-two combinations, directional control, dummies, and quick steps.

**Tactical Objectives:** Forward passes, body shape, "fake" to take opponents out of the game (move to receive, dummy, and then make next movement to receive), checking away to escape markers, and support play.

**Description (10 yard triangle):**

- A passes to B1, who lets the ball run through his legs (fake to pass/dummy).

- B2 plays a short "give and go" with B1 as shown (B2 runs around cone for return).

- B2 passes towards C1, and the same sequence is repeated in the other two points of the triangle, as shown.

- D1 completes the sequence with the pass to D2, who then becomes Player A as the circuit practice continues.

- **Player Movement Sequence:**
  A → B1 → B2 → C1 → C2 → D1 → D2 → A.

**Source:** Unai Emery's Training Session with Sevilla FC (2013)

# 10. Triangle Support Play with Lay-Offs and Third Man Runs

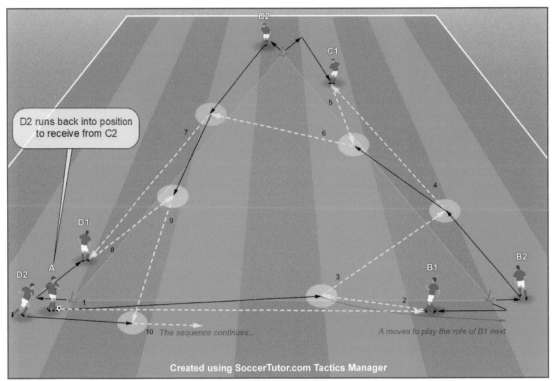

D2 runs back into position to receive from C2

The sequence continues...

A moves to play the role of B1 next

Created using SoccerTutor.com Tactics Manager

**General Objectives:** Passing and receiving within the key triangle shape, fast one-two combinations, timing of runs, and reading of various game situations.

**Players:** 9-10 (2-3 extra players).

**Technical Objectives (1/2 touches):** Passing and receiving, one-two combinations, directional control, dummies, and fast runs/movements.

**Tactical Objectives:** Forward passes, body shape, support play, checking away from markers, lay-off passes, and incisive (well-timed) third man runs.

**Description (10 yard triangle):**

- A passes to B1 and moves to receive the return pass. A then passes for the third man run of B2 off the cone.

- B2 passes forward to C1, who moves forward then back to receive. B2 moves forward to receive the lay-off and pass for the third man run of C2.

- The same sequence is repeated with C2 and D1. C2 completes the sequence with the pass to D2, who then becomes Player A as the circuit practice continues.

- **Player Movement Sequence:**
  A → B1 → B2 → C1 → C2 → D1 → D2 → A.

**Source:** Unai Emery's Training Session with Sevilla FC (2013)

**PASSING WARM-UPS**

# DIEGO SIMEONE

## Technical-Tactical Passing Warm-ups

# DIEGO SIMEONE: PROFILE

## COACHING ROLES

- **Atlético Madrid** (2011 - Present)
- **Racing Club** (2011)
- **Catalania** (2011)
- **San Lorenzo** (2009 - 2010)
- **River Plate** (2007 - 2008)
- **Estudiantes La Plata** (2006 - 2007)
- **Racing Club** (2006)

## HONOURS (Europe)

- **UEFA Europa League x 2** (2012, 2018)
- **UEFA Champions League Runner-up x 2** (2014, 2016)
- **UEFA Super Cup x 2** (2012, 2018)

## HONOURS (Domestic Leagues)

- **Spanish La Liga Primera División x 2** (2014, 2021)
- Argentine Primera División **x 2** (2006, 2008)

## HONOURS (Domestic Cups)

- **Spanish Copa del Rey** (2013)
- **Supercopa de España** (2014)

## INDIVIDUAL AWARDS

- **IFFHS Club Coach of the Decade** (2011-2020)
- **IFFHS World's Best Club Coach** (2016)
- **European Coach of the Season** (2012)
- **La Liga Coach of the Year x 3** (2013, 2014, 2016)
- **Miguel Muñoz Trophy x 2** (2014, 2016)
- **Globe Soccer Master Coach Special Award** (2017)

# 1. Creating Space to Receive in a "Y Shape" Passing Circuit

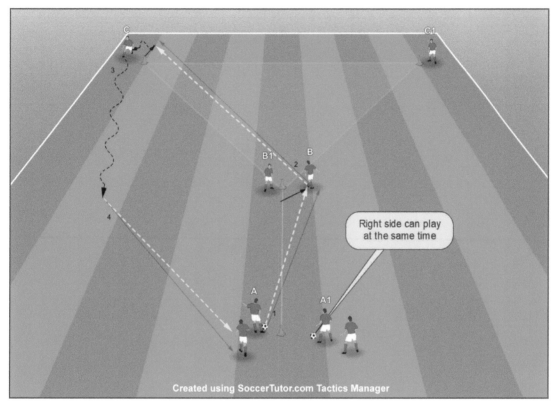

Right side can play at the same time

Created using SoccerTutor.com Tactics Manager

**General Objectives:** Improving "game timing" within the key tactical Y Shape, choice of different movements to check away from markers (up, down, across), all through various micro-game situations.

**Players:** 10-12 (2-4 extra players).

**Technical Objectives (1/2 touches):** Passing and receiving, directed control (first touch), opening up, accurate passing, and running with the ball.

**Tactical Objectives:** Body shape, decision making, checking away in different ways, creating angles, and support play.

**Description (10 yard line / 12 yard triangle):**

- A passes to B, who communicates which side to play the pass (right in diagram). B moves away from the cone, opens up, and passes diagonally to C.

- C moves forward off cone to receive, opens up, takes a directional first touch around the cone, then runs with the ball.

- C passes to the next player at the start position (A) and the same sequence is repeated with C1.

- **Player Movement Sequence:** A → B, B → C, C → A.

---

**Source:** Diego Simeone's Training Session with Atlético Madrid (2017)

**PASSING WARM-UPS**

# 2. Creating Space, Forward Run to Receive Return Pass + "Give and Go"

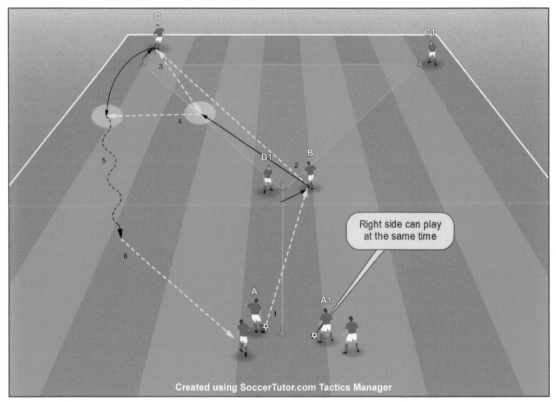

Right side can play at the same time

Created using SoccerTutor.com Tactics Manager

**General Objectives:** Improving "game timing" within the key tactical Y Shape, choice of different movements to check away from markers (up, down, across), all through various micro-game situations.

**Players:** 10-12 (2-4 extra players).

**Technical Objectives (1/2 touches):** Passing and receiving, directed control (first touch), weight of pass, receiving on the move, and running with the ball.

**Tactical Objectives:** Body shape, decision making, checking away in different ways, creating angles, and support play.

**Description (10 yard line / 12 yard triangle):**

- A passes to B, who calls out the side and checks away from the cone, opens up, and passes diagonally to C.

- C moves forward off the cone and lays the ball back for the diagonal forward run of B. B passes into the path of C to run onto (give and go around the cone).

- C runs with he ball and passes to the next player waiting. The same sequence is then repeated using A1, B1, and C1.

- **Player Movement Sequence:**
  A → B, B → C, C → A.

**Source:** Diego Simeone's Training Session with Atlético Madrid (2017)

**PASSING WARM-UPS**

# 3. Double One-Two, Long Pass, Third Man Run, and "Give and "Go"

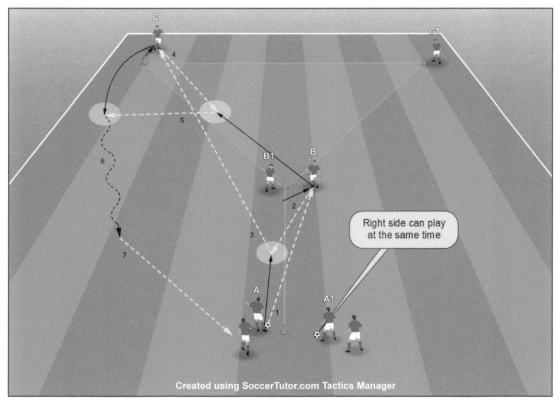

**General Objectives:** Improving "game timing" within the key tactical Y Shape, choice of different movements to check away from markers (up, down, across), all through various micro-game situations.

**Players:** 10-12 (2-4 extra players).

**Technical Objectives (1/2 touches):** Passing and receiving, directed control (first touch), one-twos, support pass, through pass, and ball control.

**Tactical Objectives:** Body shape, decision making, checking away in different ways, creating angles, and support play.

**Description (10 yard line / 12 yard triangle):**

- B calls out the side and moves off the cone - A plays a one-two with him.

- A plays a long forward pass to C, who moves forward off the cone.

- C lays the ball back for B's diagonal third man run. B passes into the path of C to run onto (give and go around the cone).

- C runs with he ball and passes to the next player waiting. The same sequence is then repeated using A1, B1, and C1.

- **Player Movement Sequence:**
  A → B, B → C, C → A.

**Source:** Diego Simeone's Training Session with Atlético Madrid (2017)

# 4. Deep Forward Pass, Lay-Off for Third Man Run, and "Give and Go"

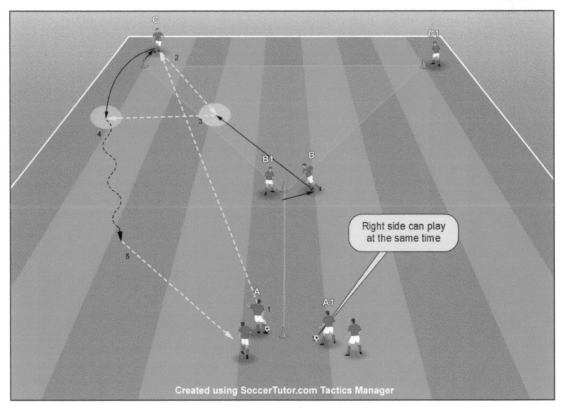

Right side can play at the same time

Created using SoccerTutor.com Tactics Manager

**General Objectives:** Timing of checking away and movements to receive, synchronised runs, and combination play.

**Players:** 10-12 (2-4 extra players).

**Technical Objectives (1/2 touches):** Passing and receiving, directed control (first touch), one-twos, support pass, through pass, and ball control.

**Tactical Objectives:** Body shape, decision making, checking away in different ways, creating angles, and support play.

**Description (10 yard line / 12 yard triangle):**

- A plays a long forward pass to C, who moves forward off the cone.

- C lays the ball back for B's diagonal third man run. B passes into the path of C to run onto (around the cone) to complete a give and go.

- C runs with he ball and passes to the next player waiting. The same sequence is then repeated using A1, B1, and C1.

- **Player Movement Sequence:**
  A → B, B → C, C → A.

---

**Source:** Diego Simeone's Training Session with Atlético Madrid (2017)

**PASSING WARM-UPS**

# 5. "Double Triangle" Combinations with Different Movements to Receive

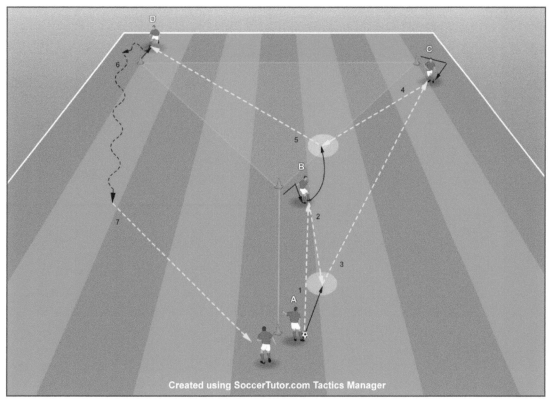

Created using SoccerTutor.com Tactics Manager

**General Objectives:** Timing of checking away and movements to receive, synchronised runs, and combination play.

**Players:** 7-9 (2-4 extra players).

**Technical Objectives (1/2 touches):** Passing and receiving, first check away, directed control (first touch), one-twos, support pass, through pass, and ball control.

**Tactical Objectives:** Body shape, decision making, checking away in different ways, creating angles, support play, switch of play, and breaking lines.

**Description (10 yard line / 12 yard triangle):**

- B checks and drops back to one side. A plays a one-two with B and then plays a long diagonal pass to C, who also checks and drops back to receive.

- C passes back for the forward movement of B, who then passes across to D.

- D has moved forward, then opens up, takes a directional touch around the cone, and runs with the ball. D passes to the next player waiting at the start.

- **Player Movement Sequence:**
  A → B, B → C, C → D, D → A.

**Source:** Diego Simeone's Training Session with Atlético Madrid (2017)

# 6. "Double Triangle" Combinations with "Give and Go" & Third Man Run

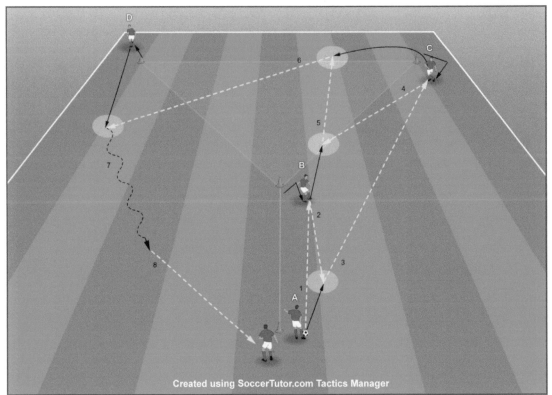

Created using SoccerTutor.com Tactics Manager

**General Objectives:** Timing of checking away and movements to receive, synchronised runs, and combination play.

**Players:** 7-9 (2-4 extra players).

**Technical Objectives (1/2 touches):** Passing and receiving, first check away, directed control (first touch), one-twos, support pass, through pass, and ball control.

**Tactical Objectives:** Body shape, decision making, checking away in different ways, creating angles, support play, holding/ timing of runs, incisive runs into space.

**Description (10 yard line / 12 yard triangle):**

- B checks and drops back to one side. A plays a one-two with B and then plays a long diagonal pass to C, who also checks and drops back to receive.

- C passes back for the forward movement of B, who plays a return pass (give and go with run around the cone).

- C plays an incisive angled pass into the path of D's third man run. D receives, runs with the ball, and passes to the start.

- **Player Movement Sequence:**
  A → B, B → C, C → D, D → A.

---

**Source:** Diego Simeone's Training Session with Atlético Madrid (2017)

# 7. "Double Triangle" Combinations with Forward Movement to Receive

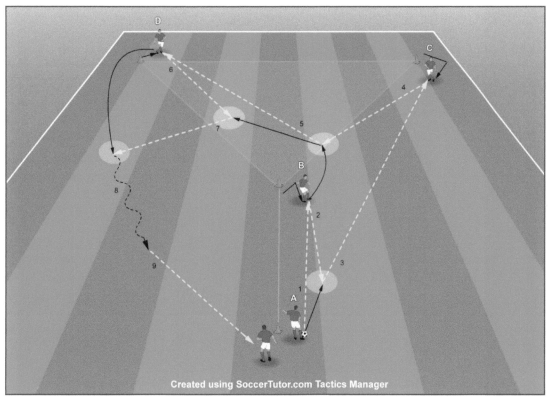

Created using SoccerTutor.com Tactics Manager

**General Objectives:** Timing of checking away and movements to receive, synchronised runs, and combination play.

**Players:** 7-9 (2-4 extra players).

**Technical Objectives (1/2 touches):** Passing and receiving, first check away, directed control (first touch), one-twos, support pass, through pass, and ball control.

**Tactical Objectives:** Body shape, decision making, different movement to receive, support play, holding/timing of runs, overlap runs, and incisive movement into space.

**Description (10 yard line/12 yard triangle):**

- B checks and drops back to one side. A plays a one-two with B and then plays a long diagonal pass to C, who also checks and drops back to receive.

- C passes back for the forward movement of B, who then plays a one-two with D, timing his second movement well to play the return (give and go around the cone).

- D receives, runs with the ball, and passes to the next player waiting at the start.

- **Player Movement Sequence:** A → B, B → C, C → D, D → A.

**Source:** Diego Simeone's Training Session with Atlético Madrid (2017)

# 8. Pass and Receive High Up with Double One-Two and "Give and Go"

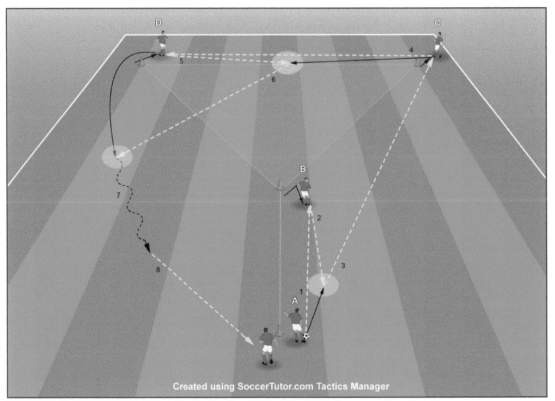

Created using SoccerTutor.com Tactics Manager

**General Objectives:** Passing and receiving, improving "game timing" within the key the tactical Y Shape, possession of the ball with good support play, all supported inside a micro-game situation.

**Players:** 7-9 (2-4 extra players).

**Technical Objectives (1/2 touches):** Passing and receiving, directed control (first touch), one-twos, support pass, through pass, and ball control.

**Tactical Objectives:** Body shape, decision making, wide and forward support play.

**Description (10 yard line / 12 yard triangle):**

- B checks and drops back to one side. A plays a one-two with B and then plays a long diagonal pass to C.

- C passes across to D, moves to meet the return, and then plays an angled pass into the path of D, who makes a run around the cone.

- D receives, runs with the ball, and passes to the next player waiting at the start.

- **Player Movement Sequence:**
  A → B, B → C, C → D, D → A.

---

**Source:** Diego Simeone's Training Session with Atlético Madrid (2017)

　　　　　　　　　　　　**PASSING WARM-UPS**

# 9. Support with Forward Movement to Receive and "Give and Go"

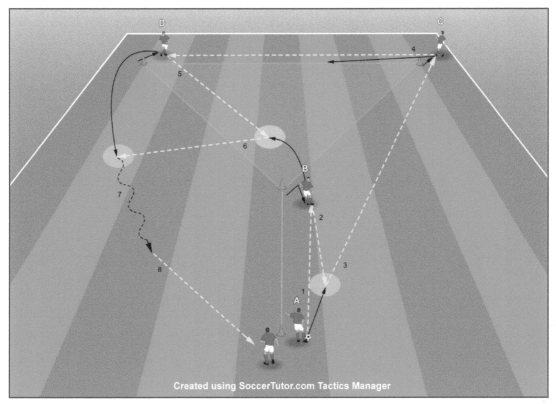

**General Objectives:** Passing and receiving, improving "game timing" within the key tactical Y Shape, possession of the ball with good support play, all supported inside a micro-game situation.

**Players:** 7-9 (2-4 extra players).

**Technical Objectives (1/2 touches):** Passing and receiving, directed control (first touch), one-twos, support pass, through pass, and ball control.

**Tactical Objectives:** Body shape, decision making, wide and forward support play.

**Description (10 yard line/12 yard triangle):**

- B checks and drops back to one side. A plays a one-two with B and then plays a long diagonal pass to C.

- C passes across to D, who lays the ball back for the forward run of B.

- D runs around the cone and B plays into his path to complete the give and go.

- D receives, runs with the ball, and passes to the next player waiting at the start.

- **Player Movement Sequence:**
  A → B, B → C, C → D, D → A.

---

**Source:** Diego Simeone's Training Session with Atlético Madrid (2017)

# 10. Complex Sequence of Checking Away and Movements to Receive

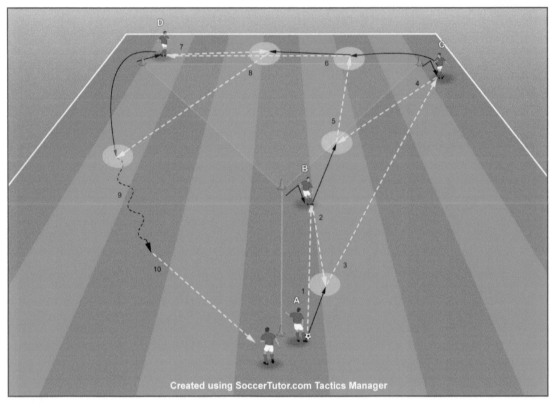

*Created using SoccerTutor.com Tactics Manager*

**General Objectives:** Passing and receiving, improving "game timing" within the key tactical Y Shape, possession of the ball with support from player without the ball (third man) and player with the ball (give and go), all in one micro-game situation.

**Players:** 7-9 (2-4 extra players).

**Technical Objectives (1/2 touches):** Passing and receiving, directed control (first touch), one-twos, support pass, through pass, and ball control.

**Tactical Objectives:** Body shape, decision making, wide and forward support play.

**Description (10 yard line / 12 yard triangle):**

- A plays a one-two with B and passes to C.

- C plays the ball back for the run of B. C runs around the cone and B plays into his path to complete the give and go.

- C plays a one-two with D and times his second movement well to play the next incisive angled pass (to complete D's give and go around the cone).

- D receives, runs with the ball, and passes to the next player at the start.

- **Player Movement Sequence:**
  A → B, B → C, C → D, D → A.

**Source:** Diego Simeone's Training Session with Atlético Madrid (2017)

# JUPP HEYNCKES

## Technical-Tactical Passing Warm-ups

# JUPP HEYNCKES: PROFILE

## COACHING ROLES

- **Bayern Munich** (2017 - 2018)
- **Bayern Munich** (2011 - 2013)
- **Bayer Leverkusen** (2009 - 2011)
- **Borussia Mönchengladbach** (2006 - 2007)
- **Schalke 04** (2003 - 2004)
- **Athletic Bilbao** (2001 - 2003)
- **Benfica** (2011 - 2013)
- **Real Madrid** (1999 – 2000)
- **Tenerife** (1995 – 1997)
- **Eintracht Frankfurt** (1994 – 1995)
- **Athletic Bilbao** (1992 - 1994)
- **Bayern Munich** (1987 - 1991)

## HONOURS (Europe)

- **UEFA Champions League x 2** (1998, 2013)
- **UEFA Champions League Runner-up** (2012)
- **UEFA Intertoto Cup x 2** (2003, 2004)

## HONOURS (Domestic Leagues)

- **German Bundesliga x 4** (1989, 1990, 2013, 2018)

## HONOURS (Domestic Leagues)

- **German DFB-Pokal** (2013)
- **German DFL-Supercup x 3** (1987, 1990, 2012)
- **Supercopa de España** (1997)

## INDIVIDUAL AWARDS

- **FIFA World Coach of the Year** (2013)
- **IFFHS World's Best Club Coach** (2013)
- **European Coach of Year - Alf Ramsey Award** (2013)
- **European Coach of the Season** (2013)
- **World Soccer Awards Manager of the Year** (2013)
- **France Football Magazine 25th Greatest Manager of All Time** (2019)
- **German Football Manager of the Year x 2** (2013, 2018)

**PASSING WARM-UPS**

# 1. Switches of Play and Finding Third Man in a Rhombus Passing Circuit

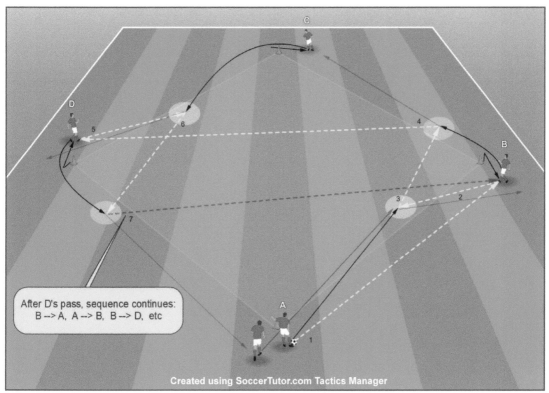

After D's pass, sequence continues:
B --> A, A --> B, B --> D, etc

Created using SoccerTutor.com Tactics Manager

**General Objectives:** Passing and receiving within the key rhombus shape, support play positioning, switching play, and scanning for the third man.

**Players:** 10-12 (2-4 extra players).

**Technical Objectives (1/2 touches):** Passing, receiving, directional first touch, ball control, support passes, and through passes.

**Tactical Objectives:** Body shape, checking away to receive, and support play with wide and forward passing.

**Description (10 yard rhombus):**

- A passes to B (who drops back) and moves forward to meet the return. B runs around the cone to receive back from A and passes across to D, who moves forward off the cone.

- C checks one way (to his left) and then makes an opposite run around the cone to receive D's lay-off. D runs around the cone (overlap) to receive back from C.

- D passes to position B. The next player waiting at A moves to receive as shown.

- **Player Movement Sequence:**
  A → B, B → C, C → D, D → A.

**Source:** Jupp Heynckes's Training Sessions with Bayern Munich (2017)

# 2. Drop and Shift Across in a Double Mirrored Rhombus with Two Balls

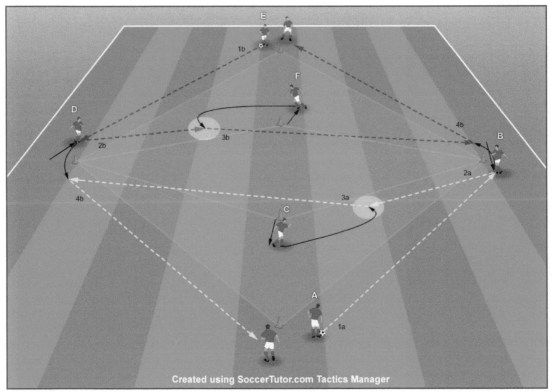

Created using SoccerTutor.com Tactics Manager

**General Objectives:** Passing and receiving within the key rhombus shape, support play positioning, switching play, and scanning for the third man.

**Players:** 10-12 (2-4 extra players).

**Technical Objectives (1/2 touches):** Passing, receiving, directional first touch, ball control, support passes, and through passes.

**Tactical Objectives:** Body shape, checking away to receive, and support play with wide and forward passing.

**Description (2 x 10 yard rhombuses):**

- There are 2 balls, and the same pattern is played simultaneously on both mirrored sides - see the yellow and blue lines.

- A/E pass to B/D, who drop back to receive. C/F drop back and then make a curved run across to receive B/D's pass.

- D and B make opposite movements to receive the next passes from C and F. They complete the sequence by passing to the next players waiting at the starts.

- **Player Movement Sequence:**
  A → B, B → C, C → D, D → E, E→ F, F → A.

**Source:** Jupp Heynckes's Training Sessions with Bayern Munich (2017)

**PASSING WARM-UPS**

# 3. Switch of Play in a Double Mirrored Rhombus with Two Balls

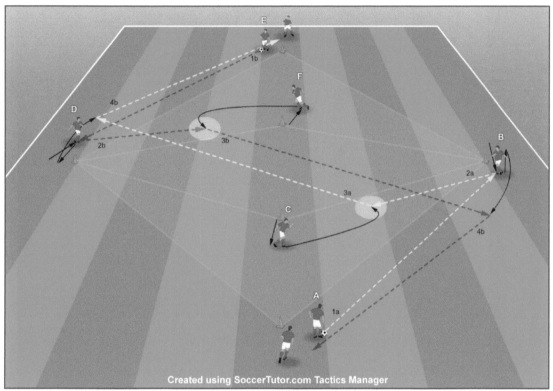

Created using SoccerTutor.com Tactics Manager

**General Objectives:** Passing and receiving within the key rhombus shape, support play positioning, switching play (playing for the cutting run on the opposite side).

**Players:** 10-12 (2-4 extra players).

**Technical Objectives (1/2 touches):** Passing, receiving, directional first touch, ball control, support passes, and through passes.

**Tactical Objectives:** Body shape, checking away to receive, and support play with wide and forward passing.

**Description (2 x 10 yard rhombuses):**

- This is a variation of the practice on the previous page.

- A/E pass to B/D, who drop back to receive. C/F drop back and then make a curved run across to receive B/D's pass.

- **Variation:** C/F pass to B/D on the opposite side of their cone compared to the practice on the previous page *(134)*. B passes back to Position E and D back to Position A. The practice continues.

- **Player Movement Sequence:**
  A → B, B → C, C → D, D → E, E→ F, F → A.

**Source:** Jupp Heynckes's Training Sessions with Bayern Munich (2017)

**PASSING WARM-UPS**

# 4. Two-Ball Double Rhombus Circuit with Opening Up and "Give and Go"

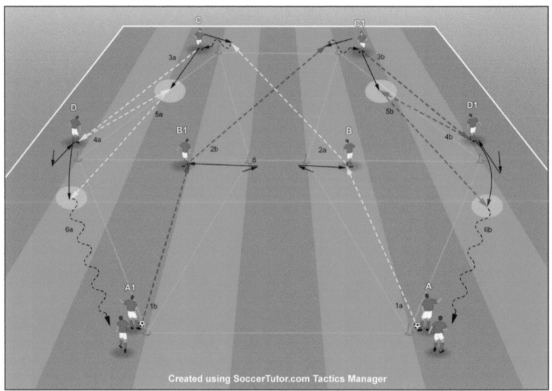

Created using SoccerTutor.com Tactics Manager

**General Objectives:** Attacking actions and combinations with quality timing (synchronised) for different movements and creating a micro-game situation.

**Players:** 14-16 (4-6 extra players).

**Technical Objectives (1/2 touches):** Passing, receiving, directional first touch, ball control, support passes, and through passes.

**Tactical Objectives:** Body shape, checking away to receive, and support play with wide and forward passing.

**Description (10 yard distances):**

- A passes to B, who checks and makes a counter-movement to receive.

- B opens up to receive and passes to C, who opens up and takes a directional touch around the cone.

- C plays a one-two with D and then passes into space. D has initially dropped back, and then made a counter-movement to receive C's pass and dribble to A1.

- **Player Movement Sequence:**
  A → B, B → C, C → D, D → A1.

- Both sides run simultaneously (mirrored).

---

**Source:** Jupp Heynckes's Training Sessions with Bayern Munich (2017)

# 5. Two-Ball Double Rhombus Circuit with One-Twos and Third Man Runs

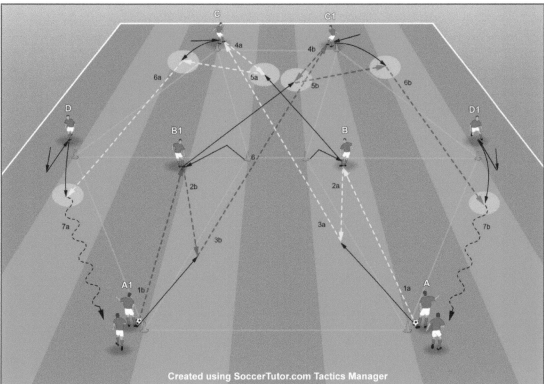

Created using SoccerTutor.com Tactics Manager

**General Objectives:** Attacking actions and combinations with quality timing (synchronised) for different movements and creating a micro-game situation.

**Players:** 14-16 (4-6 extra players).

**Technical Objectives (1/2 touches):**
Passing, receiving, directional first touch, ball control, support passes, and through passes.

**Tactical Objectives:** Body shape, checking away to receive, and support play with wide and forward passing.

**Description (10 yard distances):**

- A plays a one-two with B. A runs forward to meet the return and pass to C.

- B makes a third man run to receive C's lay-off. C runs around the cone to receive back from B (give and go).

- D has initially dropped back, and then makes a counter-movement to receive C's through pass and dribble to A1.

- **Player Movement Sequence:**
  A → B, B → C, C → D, D → A1.

- Both sides run simultaneously (mirrored).

---

**Source:** Jupp Heynckes's Training Sessions with Bayern Munich (2017)

# 6. Two-Ball Double Rhombus Circuit with Forward Runs and Overlaps

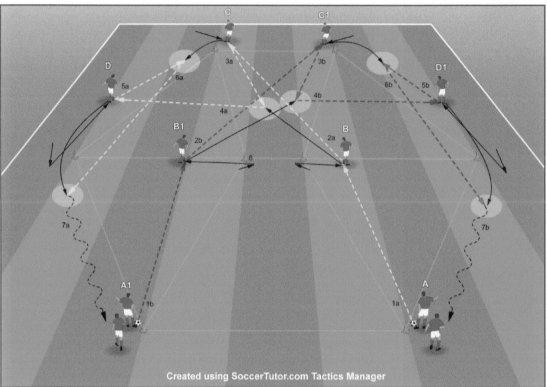

Created using SoccerTutor.com Tactics Manager

**General Objectives:** Attacking actions and combinations with quality timing (synchronised) for different movements and creating a micro-game situation.

**Players:** 14-16 (4-6 extra players).

**Technical Objectives (1/2 touches):** Passing, receiving, directional first touch, ball control, support passes, and through passes.

**Tactical Objectives:** Body shape, checking away to receive, and support play with wide and forward passing.

**Description (10 yard distances):**

- A passes to B, who checks and makes a counter-movement to receive.

- B plays a one-two with C, moving forward to meet the return. B then passes across to D, who has moved to pass back for C (who runs around cone).

- D then makes a counter-movement (overlap run around cone) to receive C's through pass and dribble to the start.

- **Player Movement Sequence:**
  A → B, B → C, C → D, D → A1.

- Both sides run simultaneously (mirrored).

**Source:** Jupp Heynckes's Training Sessions with Bayern Munich (2017)

**PASSING WARM-UPS**

# 7. Open Up, Receive, Pass in Central Rhombus + "Give and Go" Overlap

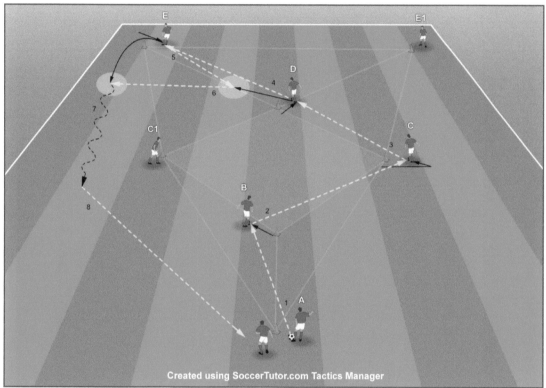

Created using SoccerTutor.com Tactics Manager

**General Objectives:** Passing and receiving within the key rhombus shape, attacking actions/combinations with quality timing (synchronised) for different movements and creating a micro-game situation.

**Players:** 12-14 (4-6 extra players).

**Technical Objectives (1/2 touches):** Passing, receiving, directional first touch, ball control, support passes, and through passes.

**Tactical Objectives:** Body shape, checking away to receive, and support play with wide and forward passing.

**Description (10 yard distances):**

- A passes to B, who moves off the cone and opens up to receive. B passes to C, who checks, moves, and passes to D.

- D moves off the cone and passes to E.

- E moves one way to receive and then plays a give and go with D, running around the cone to receive the return.

- E runs with the ball and passes to the next player waiting (position A) - the sequence repeats using C1 and E1.

- **Player Movement Sequence:**
  A → B, B → C, C → D, D → E, E → A.

**Source:** Jupp Heynckes's Training Sessions with Bayern Munich (2017)

139

# 8. Double Support Play in Central Rhombus + "Give and Go" Overlap

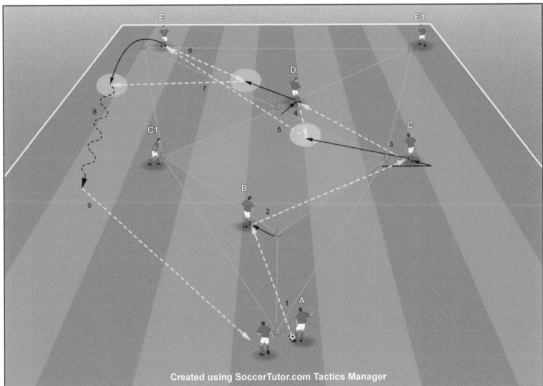

Created using SoccerTutor.com Tactics Manager

**General Objectives:** Passing and receiving within the key rhombus shape, attacking actions/combinations with quality timing (synchronised) for different movements, and creating a micro-game situation.

**Players:** 12-14 (4-6 extra players).

**Technical Objectives (1/2 touches):** Passing, receiving, directional first touch, ball control, support passes, and through passes.

**Tactical Objectives:** Body shape, checking away to receive, and support play with wide and forward passing.

**Description (10 yard distances):**

- A passes to B, who moves off the cone and opens up to receive. B passes to C, who checks, moves, and passes to D.

- D moves off the cone and lays the ball off for the inside run of C, who passes to E.

- D moves across and E plays a give and go with him - E runs around cone, controls the pass, and runs with the ball.

- E passes to the next player waiting and the sequence repeats using C1 and E1.

- **Player Movement Sequence:**
  A → B, B → C, C → D, D → E, E → A.

**Source:** Jupp Heynckes's Training Sessions with Bayern Munich (2017)

**PASSING WARM-UPS**

# 9. Triple One-Two with Forward Pass (Open Up) + "Give and Go" Overlap

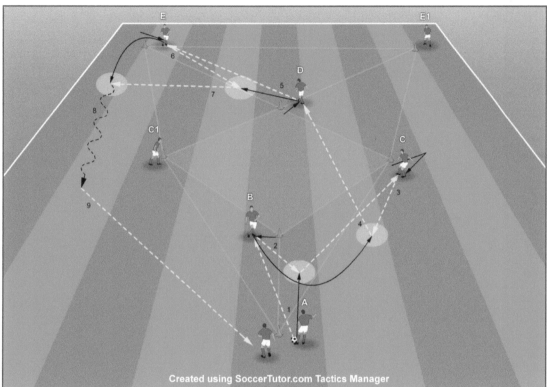

Created using SoccerTutor.com Tactics Manager

**General Objectives:** Passing and receiving within the key rhombus shape, attacking actions/combinations with quality timing (synchronised) for different movements, and creating a micro-game situation.

**Players:** 12-14 (4-6 extra players).

**Technical Objectives (1/2 touches):** Passing, receiving, directional first touch, ball control, support passes, and through passes.

**Tactical Objectives:** Body shape, checking away to receive, and support play with wide and forward passing.

**Description (10 yard distances):**

- A plays a one-two with B.

- A then plays a one-two with C before passing forward to D, who opens up to receive and passes to E.

- E moves one way to receive and plays a give and go with D, running around the cone to receive the return.

- E runs with the ball and passes to the next player waiting (position A) - the sequence repeats using C1 and E1.

- **Player Movement Sequence:**
  A → B, B → C, C → D, D → E, E → A.

**Source:** Jupp Heynckes's Training Sessions with Bayern Munich (2018)

**PASSING WARM-UPS**

# 10. Different Runs to Receive Lay-Offs + "Give and Go" Overlap

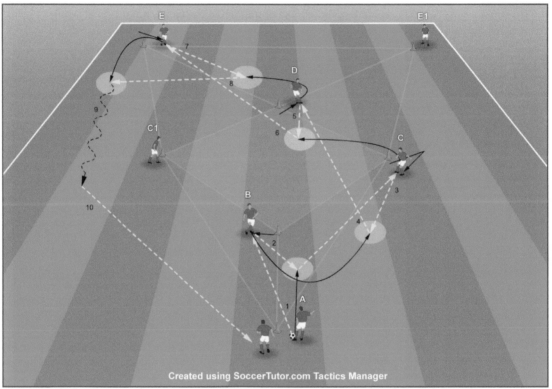

Created using SoccerTutor.com Tactics Manager

**General Objectives:** Passing and receiving within the key rhombus shape, attacking actions/combinations with quality timing (synchronised) for different movements, and creating a micro-game situation.

**Players:** 12-14 (4-6 extra players).

**Technical Objectives (1/2 touches):** Passing, receiving, directional first touch, ball control, support passes, and through passes.

**Tactical Objectives:** Body shape, checking away to receive, and support play with wide and forward passing.

**Description (10 yard distances):**

- A plays a one-two with B. A then plays a one-two with C before passing forward to D - he lays the ball back for C, who runs around the cone to receive.

- C passes to E and D moves to meet the next pass. E plays a give and go with D (running around the cone), controls the return pass, and runs with the ball.

- E passes to the next player waiting and the sequence repeats using C1 and E1.

- **Player Movement Sequence:**
  A → B, B → C, C → D, D → E, E → A.

---

**Source:** Jupp Heynckes's Training Sessions with Bayern Munich (2018)

**PASSING WARM-UPS**

# BIBLIOGRAPHY

- K. P. Knebel, B. Herbeck, G. Hamsen, "La ginnastica funzionale nella preparazione del calciatore", Società Stampa Sportiva, Roma 1993.

- E. Arcelli, F. Ferretti, "Preparazione Atletica", Edizioni Sport Italia, 1993.

- E. Arcelli, "Che cos'è l'allenamento", Sperling & Kupfer", 1990.

- N. Comucci, G. Leali, "L'allenamento di condizione per il calciatore", Società Stampa Sportiva, Roma 2000.

- A. Cei, "Psicologia dello sport", Il Mulino, Bologna 1998.

- R. Nicoletti, A. M. Borghi, "Il controllo motorio", Il Mulino, Bologna 2007.

- Settore Giovanile Scolastico F.I.G.C., "Guida tecnica per le scuole calcio", Roma 2003.

- R. Schmidt, A, Wrinsberg, "Apprendimento motorio e Prestazione", Società Stampa Sportiva, Roma 2003.

- F. Garcea, "Il manuale della tecnica calcistica", Allenatore.net, Bozzano (LU) 2004.

- F. Garcea, "Il calcio: conoscerlo per insegnarlo", Allenatore.net, Bozzano (LU) 2006.

- F. Garcea, T. Lorito, "Calcio giovanile; lo sguardo di un allenatore e di uno psicologo", Edizioni ETS, Pisa 2007.

- F. Garcea, M. Cacicia, F. Macri, "Il calcio: conoscerlo per insegnarlo", Allenatore.net, Bozzano (LU) 2008.

- F. Garcea, S. Becchi, "Allenare la lettura degli spazi", Allenatore.net, Bozzano (LU) 2017.

- M. Lucchesi, "Organizzazione Geometrica", Allenatore.net, Bozzano (LU) 2013.

- Articoli di F. Garcea tratti da www.allenatore.net

- Bayern Munich Training Camp in Riva del Garda, 2015.

- Napoli Training Camp in Dimaro, 2017.

- Napoli Training Camp in Dimaro, 2018.

- Visit of Real Madrid Sports City, 2014.

- Visit of Bayern Munich's Training Ground (Säbener Straße), 2015.

- Visit of Torre del Grifo Village (Training Centre of Calcio Catania), 2011.

- Visit of Camp des Loges (Paris Saint-Germain F.C. Training Ground), 2017.

- Atlético de Madrid YouTube Channel (2016-2018) - Available at: https://www.youtube.com/channel/UCuzKFwdh7z2GHcIOX_tXgxA [Accessed 2017-2018]

- Bayern Munich YouTube Channel (2015-2018) - Available at: https://www.youtube.com/user/fcbayern [Accessed 2017-2018]

- Bayern Munich YouTube Channel (2015-2018)
  - Available at: https://www.youtube.com/user/fcbayern [Accessed 2017-2018]

- Manchester City YouTube Channel (2017-2018)
  - Available at: https://www.youtube.com/channel/UCkzCjdRMrW2vXLx8mvPVLdQ [Accessed 2017-2018]

- Sevilla YouTube Channel (2013)
  - Available at: https://www.youtube.com/user/SEVILLAFC [Accessed 2017-2018]

- UEFA YouTube Channel (2017)
  - Available at: https://www.youtube.com/channel/UCyGa1YEx9ST66rYrJTGIKOw [Accessed 2017-2018]

I have a special thank you to my father who has not been around for a long time, to my mother, to my family, to the women of my life, Valeria, and to the little Noemi and Viola.

Thanks go to all the companies, to the executives who believed in my philosophy, in my ideas, in my concepts, in my principles and in my abilities.

Thanks to all the players I have trained, as thanks to you I have acquired self-awareness, experience, trust, and security, I learned to keep relationships, compare, experiment, edit and expand my knowledge.

Thanks to Martino Melis, a friendship born on the first school desks and on the football fields after.

A special thanks to Maurizio and Marcello Pantani and the whole Pantani family for having always demonstrated their trust and esteem.

Thanks to all the members of the U.S. Città di Pontedera who helped me realise the dream of obtain the UEFA A diploma and become a professional coach.

Thanks to the municipal administration of Pontedera, in particular to Mayor Millozzi and to the Franconi Sports Councilor for always being available and close to the U.S. Città di Pontedera and the youth sector of the U.S. Città di Pontedera.

Thanks to Elio Ferri and Luca Franceschi (AS Roma) who asked me to start more than 20 years ago to coach the football school in my country.

Thanks to Luciano Spalletti (Inter coach) and all his staff.

Thanks to Marco Domenichini (Coach in Inter 2nd team), who has always been close to me since I started all my adventures.

Thanks to Massimiliano Cappellini, Moreno Simonetti, Fausto Garcea and Antonio Cernicchiaro, for me you are like a second family.

Thanks to Vito Consoloni, Sergio Giuntini, and Alessandro Balluchi.

Thanks to Vincent my spiritual "guru," to Giovanna Catizone, VinceJr and Alessandra for the fantastic experience, to Eddie Rossman my football brother from Staten Island (New York), to Joe Correale, Cosimo, Rosemarie, Maryann, Anthony, Alyssa for all they have made for me. To the president coaches, Renzo Ulivieri, a man who with his football passion makes his lectures to the teachers he teaches unique, extraordinary, and indescribable. They passed on their experiences, skills, and knowledge throughout the UEFA A course at Coverciano Federal Technical Centre, which is the best coaching school in the world.

**Daniele Zini**

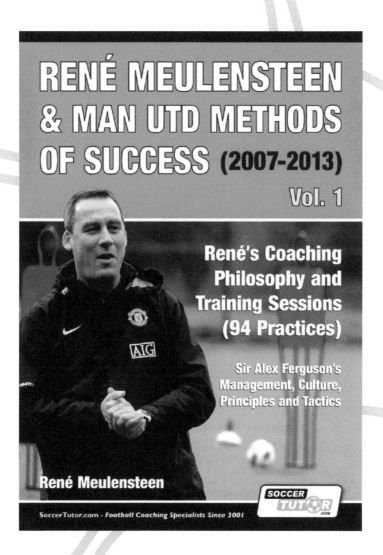

Lightning Source UK Ltd.
Milton Keynes UK
UKHW050410221122
412586UK00005B/37